GLIMPSES OF HOPE —
GOD BEYOND GROUND ZERO

ON REFLECTION SERIES

# Glimpses of Hope —
# God Beyond Ground Zero

Johnston McKay

Series Editor:
Duncan B Forrester

SAINT ANDREW PRESS
EDINBURGH

First published in 2002 by
SAINT ANDREW PRESS
121 George Street, Edinburgh EH2 4YN

ISBN 0 7152 0801 2

The right of Johnston McKay to be identified as author of this work has been asserted
in accordance with the Copyright, Designs and Patents Act 1988.

The authorial views expressed in this book are those of Johnston McKay alone. The
opinions expressed by the author and his interviewees do not represent the official
views of the Church of Scotland, which can be laid down only by the General Assembly.

While every effort has been made to verify the accuracy of previously published
quotations and to obtain permissions where appropriate, the author will be pleased to
rectify any omissions for future editions of this book.

**British Library Cataloguing in Publication Data**
A catalogue record for this book is available from the British Library.

Typeset in Times by Pioneer Associates, Perthshire

Printed and bound in the United Kingdom by
Creative Print & Design, Wales

# Contents

# Foreword

IT is a great pleasure to contribute a foreword to Johnston McKay's latest book. I am pleased for friendship's sake, and I am pleased because it is an exceptionally good book – moving and intelligent and surprisingly (for a book of real theology) beautiful.

For over thirty years, the author and I have been friends. It is not easy to be a friend of Johnston McKay – for at least two reasons. The first is that he takes great delight in arguing – and no-one does it better. So, to be his friend can be fairly demanding. The second is that he has read everything: whenever I recommend a book to him, he has read it and can point out to me weaknesses I had not observed. Despite these flaws, however, he is the kindest of friends. And he is an outstanding writer, broadcaster and preacher.

After the attack on the World Trade Center, Johnston went to New York and made radio programmes. Anyone who heard these programmes will not forget them. So I am immensely grateful that some of the insights and stories which made these programmes so powerful emerge in this book. He has the true broadcaster's ear for the chance remark, the odd coincidence which illuminates the whole scene; and he has the true philosopher's nose for the meaning which lies behind the apparent oddness, the seeming coincidence.

He writes and speaks the way he thinks: never aggressive, never simplistic, always suggestive, often winsome. Throughout this book, he wrestles with the deepest questions about God, and in particular – how could it be otherwise after September 11th? – with the question of God and evil. Johnston McKay's understanding of Christian thinking is subtle, but his grasp of the central message of the gospel is sure.

Johnston is very fond of the work of the Welsh poet R. S. Thomas. One of Thomas's most famous poems is 'The Country Clergy':

> They left no books,
> Memorial to their lonely thought
> In grey parishes; rather they wrote
> On men's hearts and in the minds
> Of young children sublime words
> Too soon forgotten. God in his time
> Or out of time will correct this.

It is a very good thing indeed that the words which Johnston McKay has spoken and written in the hearts and minds of his listeners are now available to all.

Andrew McLellan
(Moderator of the General Assembly, 2000–1)

# Preface

TWO months after the attack on the Twin Towers in Lower
Manhattan on September 11th 2001, I went with two colleagues,
Anna Magnusson and Erica Morrison, to record four reflections
for Advent at and about what had become known as Ground
Zero. These were later edited and crafted by a third producer,
Mo McCullough, who has been my outstandingly creative
colleague and close friend since I joined the BBC in 1987.

I also recorded four conversations which were transmitted in
a series I present on BBC Radio Scotland called *Personal
Touch*, produced by Anna.

For the past ten years, I have led Holy Week meditations in
Houston and Killellan Parish Church, Renfrewshire, Scotland.
Usually what I have said has included references to current
events, but it was impossible in Holy Week in the year 2002 not
to reflect on the events of September 11th in the previous year.

The Introduction and the first six chapters of this book are
based on the programmes I recorded and the Holy Week
meditations I led. While I owe a very large debt to the three
producers I have mentioned, it would be very unfair not to
include in my thanks our other colleagues Catriona Murray,
Ailsa MacIntosh and Tom Dunlop. As I write this, I have retire-
ment from full-time work with the BBC in my sights. No-one
could have had a more talented team to lead nor more loyal
friends to work with. Nor could any preacher wish for a more
supportive congregation than the people of Houston and

Killellan, well and often bravely led by the Rev. Georgie Baxendale.

As the journalist Aaron Hicklin pointed out in a conversation with him which is quoted in these pages, the story of September 11th has changed and will continue to change as time goes by. So I have included in this book versions of meditations and reflections given to congregations or broadcast since Easter 2002, when the themes of worship as well as the Christian calendar moved on too.

Alison Elliot has read this book at every stage of its development. As well as pointing out where the language was unclear, she has made comments which made me think again about what I wanted to say. Her interest in the book and her constant support have mattered very much to me, as has the encouragement and friendship of Andrew McLellan, who has contributed a typically gracious foreword.

My wife Evelyn and daughter Cally have had to allow me far more time than should be my share on the family word-processor in order to allow me to complete this book. My thanks are due to them not only for that but also, much more importantly, for providing the context of love and security in which I came to know the truth I try to express in the pages which follow.

Johnston McKay
June 2002

# Introduction

ONE of the stories which reached Scotland in the days following September 11th 2001 (and, if there was no way of knowing
whether some of these stories were accurate, many of them
nevertheless had a ring of truth) was about a couple who lived
in a typically neat suburb of an American city, where there are
no fences or hedges between the green lawns that border on
the often white-painted houses. So, neighbours, cutting their
share of the long strip of grass, get to know each other and
become friendly.

The man in this story worked in the World Trade Center. He
became friendly with the neighbours, people from abroad,
who surprised him in the first week of September by saying
they had won a foreign holiday for two but were not able to take
up the prize. So they offered him the trip. Off he and his wife
went; and, when they returned shortly after September 11th,
their neighbours had vanished.

Did the offer of the foreign holiday come from one of the
conspirators? Is the story apocryphal? Or do all of us need to
believe that, even in a world of such callous inhumanity as the
attacks planned and executed on the World Trade Center, there
is still a place for a touch of kindness, goodness and sympathy?

The first part of this book tries to reflect on what happened
on September 11th in the light of what people of Christian faith
believe about the last days of Jesus of Nazareth. And, if the
story is true about conspirators who made sure their neighbour

who worked in the World Trade Center was well out of the way on September 11th, there is a parallel incident of compassionate pity in John's Gospel's account of the last hours of Jesus' life (John 19:28–9). Jesus calls out: 'I thirst'. The One who had promised that 'whoever drinks of what I shall give him' is, himself, parched. 'A jar of sour wine was standing there. So they put a sponge full of wine on a branch of hyssop, and held it to his mouth.' This is often interpreted as the soldiers' mocking of Jesus, offering him an undrinkable drink; but among Roman soldiers there was a popular drink made by mixing vinegar, water and eggs. Maybe this is what they gave to Jesus. What matters, however, is not what they gave him to drink but whether these soldiers, who could callously play dice at the foot of the cross for the tunic of the One they had crucified, could also be finally moved to pity.

We should never underestimate the importance of simple, unglamorous acts of compassion. After all, Jesus once said that God is interested even in someone who offers a cup of water to someone else. It is easy to underestimate the effect of the small gesture of compassion not only on someone going through the extreme suffering that Jesus endured on the cross but also on a person whose trials are a lot less dramatic. It breaks the cycle of apparently unrelieved pain, but it also destroys the sense of utter isolation.

The poet Edwin Muir asked the question:

If a good man were ever housed in Hell
  By needful error of the qualities,
Perhaps to prove the rule or shame the devil,
  Or speak the truth only a stranger sees,

Would he, surrendering to obvious hate
    Fill half eternity with cries and tears,
Or watch beside Hell's little wicket gate
    In patience for the first ten thousand years,

Feeling the curse climb slowly to his throat
    That, uttered, dooms him to rescindless ill,
Forcing his praying tongue to run by rote
    Eternity entire before him still?

Would he, at last, grown faithful in his station,
    Kindle a little hope in hopeless Hell,
And sow among the damned doubts of damnation,
    Since here someone could live, and could live well?

One doubt of evil would bring down such a grace,
    Open such a gate, all Eden would enter in,
Hell be a place like any other place,
    And love and hate and life and death begin.

As I hope we will see, there were more than a few good people in New York in and after September 11th who were housed in hell, and they showed that they could kindle a little hope there. For many of us, Christian faith and what it has had to say in the wake of the attacks on the Twin Towers also kindles hope in hopeless hell. But that hope is neither easy optimism nor facile cheerfulness. It is born of the sort of stories that people of faith have told about hope down through the centuries.

Three of these stories from the Hebrew Bible have been very important to me as I tried to understand what faith might say about September 11th. The first is a very primitive and, on the surface, a very brutal story. It is the story of Abraham prepared to sacrifice his son Isaac (Genesis 22:1–14) because that was what he believed God wanted him to do. Just as he was about to kill his son, Abraham looked up and saw a ram, caught in a thicket by its horns; and he offered it up as a burnt offering instead of the son who was precious to him, but whom he was prepared to sacrifice – Isaac, the son who had been born to Sarah at a miraculously old age, the son who was the proof that God kept his promises. For hadn't God promised that Abraham would be the father of a great nation? And wasn't Isaac the proof that he might yet be just that? And yet here was Abraham prepared to do what he believed God wanted him to do, even when it seemed to mean that the promise would never be fulfilled, even when it seemed that the future would no longer exist, even when it contradicted every natural human instinct.

There's no point in asking whether this incident actually happened. The writer of Genesis is dealing not with the historian's facts or the scientist's data but with the storyteller's understanding of truth. And there's no point in asking whether God really demands that fathers are prepared to sacrifice their sons on firewood gathered nearby. The writer of Genesis lived in a world which believed that human sacrifice was the most powerful and most effective sacrifice anyone could make to any God.

The story is told dramatically to make one single point: that true faith consists of being obedient even if it means having to sacrifice the future which God has promised you. We will see that that was a challenge some have had to face in the wake of September 11th.

I have never been able to believe that, when Jesus was nailed to the cross, he knew beyond all doubt what his disciples were to discover three days later. I have never been able to believe that, when Jesus died, he had 20/20 vision into the Easter future.

For, if he had, it makes that dreadful cry which Mark and Matthew both record – 'My God, my God, why have you abandoned me?' – less than real, less than the cry of dereliction which Christians have found it to be; strangely, less than the comforting cry which Christians who have felt themselves abandoned have found it to be.

Jesus died trusting God. But that's the point. Trusting God even though it seemed that God had asked him to sacrifice the future that God himself had promised. Such was the trust; and it was that incredible trust which took the death of this man Jesus out of the hands of calculating Caiaphas and prevaricating Pilate. Between them they may have sentenced Jesus to death, but by his trust Jesus made of his death something which was his. That trust robbed the murderous men who hammered in the nails of a death. It stole an execution from the cynical soldiers who supervised it all and then gambled with his last belongings. That trust denied death its power.

I do not think it is blasphemy to say that, in the stories we were told of doomed passengers on the hijacked planes contacting their loved ones by mobile phones and expressing love in the face of death, we were seeing a reflection of Jesus on Good Friday. I do not think it is sacrilege to say that, in the reports of people determined to try to wrest control of an aircraft from the hijackers, not in order to save themselves (for that was not possible) but in order to prevent carnage on the ground, something of that obedience to a future which would be denied them echoes the attitude of Jesus as he approached his death.

The second story from the Hebrew Bible that has helped me in the aftermath of September 11th tells of someone who found obedience less stark than Abraham, and so more nearly matches the attitude of most of us. Elijah, who had earned himself the proud title of 'the troubler of Israel', is on the run (1 Kings

19:1–21). He has tried to put some backbone into the spineless
King Ahab. He has aroused the fury of Ahab's Queen Jezebel,
who has vowed to have him killed. So he makes his escape; and,
after a day's exhausting journey, he collapses beside a bush and
says: 'God, I've had enough'. He journeys on and collapses
again beside a cave, and God asks of him: 'What are you doing
here?' Elijah says that, despite his preaching, his people have
abandoned their religion and slaughtered the prophets, and only
he is left. And that is when God tells Elijah to stand at the mouth
of the cave, and he will pass by. There is a raging wind, but the
Lord is not in the wind; then there is an earthquake, but the Lord
is not in the earthquake; then a fire, but the Lord is not in the
fire. And then a still small voice.

In a very perceptive book,[1] Professor Robert Davidson, a
former Church of Scotland Moderator (1990), writes: 'The Lord
was not in the wind . . . not in the earthquake . . . not in the
fire . . . *but he ought to have been*' – because, in the stories
which mattered most to the people of Israel, it was in earthquake, wind and fire that God had been used to make himself
known: when, as Deborah's song puts it (Judges 5:4–5), the
earth trembled as God prepared to rescue his people; or when,
as the Hebrew slaves fled from Pharaoh, the wind parted the
Sea of Reeds (Exodus 14:21–3); or when, in the bush that
burned but was not consumed, God appeared to Moses (Exodus
3:2–3). Robert Davidson adds: 'The traditional symbols of the
Lord's presence and activity no longer seemed to carry power
or conviction. Where [Elijah] had been taught to believe that the
Lord was present, in wind, earthquake and fire, there he found
him to be disturbingly absent. Yet the Lord was there in something that appeared to be totally different in character from what
had hitherto been comfortably familiar.'

As we will see, that too is something that has had to be faced since September 11th. One church leader in New York said that before September 11th he had never met an Imam; but, within a few weeks of September 11th, he was holding two-day retreats with several Imams as they tried to examine what God might be saying to them.

The unexpected which replaced the expected for Elijah was that still small voice, but hardly the 'still small voice of calm' of John Greenleaf Whittier's famous hymn. What this still small voice said to Elijah was to get back to the political and religious ferment from which he had escaped, to return to the very place where he had been hurt and take up precisely the work he thought he had been able to lay down. 'God, I've had enough', Elijah had said – and it was as if God replied: 'Well, I haven't!' Many people in the wake of September 11th found what they had to endure too much to put up with. Katherine Avery, the co-ordinator of rescue services at St Paul's Chapel in Lower Manhattan (which I will describe much more fully in Chapter 1) said, two months after September 11th: 'I don't think that many of us are actually dealing with what is going on. I function all day long. I manage to keep going. I don't really stop and let things sink in. At some point I know I'm going to have to do that.' And yet, day after day, week after week, she was going back to where she was going to be hurt again and again. But it shows some hope in hopeless hell when people are prepared to risk their vulnerability again and again for others, and for God.

I was reminded of a favourite story about St Teresa of Avila, the fourteenth-century Carmelite nun and spiritual writer, when she was on her way to found another of her Carmelite houses. After a list of dreadful difficulties – sore throat, temperature and much more – she arrived at a river she had to cross, only to find that a torrent had carried away all the bridges and that the only way across was to abandon her carriage and wade across.

As she did so, she shouted out: 'Lord, in the midst of all these ills, this comes on the top of the rest'; and she heard God's voice saying: 'But Teresa, that is how I treat my friends', to which Teresa replied caustically: 'Yes, my Lord, and that is why you have so few of them'.

The third passage from the Hebrew Bible comes from the Book of Jeremiah. Word reaches Jeremiah when he is in prison that a piece of land in his home village of Anathoth is for sale and, as a member of the family, he has 'first refusal'. The trouble is that, at the time when this news reaches Jeremiah, Anathoth is about seven miles behind the lines of the Babylonians who are laying siege to the country. As soon as Jeremiah gets word of this possible purchase, he decides he must buy, and what makes him reach this decision is the very fact that the land in question is occupied. It hardly comes with what estate agents call 'vacant possession'. The idea of the purchase is so absurd that Jeremiah decides that the suggestion that he buy it must be what he calls 'a word from the Lord'. Later, he explains this absurd purchase as a prophetic gesture which claims that 'houses and fields and vineyards shall again be bought in this land'.

I have believed for a long time that Christians are intended to be God's plot of land in a hostile environment, God's gesture which indicates that the future, however bleak it seems, lies with God and with his people of faith. So, how people of faith coped with the events of September 11th was not simply a matter for them. Their beliefs in the face of such evil were the equivalent of the purchase of ground far behind enemy lines, what the poet Edwin Muir describes as 'kindling hope in hope-less hell', as we have already seen. What follows is my attempt as a Christian thinker, preacher and broadcaster to contribute to the way in which Christian faith can try to express that hope.

# 1

# Living in Hope

EARLY in 1996, I took some people to the Holy Land to make a number of radio programmes. One of the programmes was recorded in the Garden of Gethsemane. Bus after bus was emptying its tourist load into the garden. In language after language, guides were explaining what happened to Jesus there. When the recording was finished, I made my way through the crowds towards the Church of All Nations next to Gethsemane, and as I approached it I saw on one of the pillars a notice which was meant to silence the tourist guides when they took their parties through the doors: 'Please, no explanations inside the Church'.

A few weeks later, I told radio listeners about the notice when I spoke the morning after the shootings in Dunblane; and I remembered it again on September 11th 2001. Like the massacre at Dunblane, or the destruction of Pan Am flight 103 over Lockerbie, both in my native Scotland, the destruction of the Twin Towers in New York raises very serious questions for people of Christian faith who must attempt to provide answers if their faith is to be at all credible. These events can lead to deep doubts which many people of Christian faith, if they are to be honest, find themselves sharing. I want to share the glimpses of answers to some of these questions which the faith of those affected provides, while sharing many of the doubts these events have raised. But I want also to share my belief that Christian faith cannot ultimately provide the sort of clear-cut

1

explanations which people expect to profoundly difficult questions; rather, the explanations Christian faith has to offer are expressed through stories, and especially through the story of the life, death and resurrection of Jesus of Nazareth.

It is often very difficult for people to accept a story as a vehicle for truth – for two reasons. First of all, they assume that stories are trivial, unimportant and childish, whereas the reality is that people have a profound need to share stories, especially in the wake of an event such as September 11th.

Rosalind Galt is a Scottish postgraduate student at Brown University in New York. Towards the end of the week of September 11th, she wrote:[2]

Everyone in the city has a World Trade Center story, and everyone you talk to tells you their story, or the story of their friends. By degrees of separation you hear so many narratives, spread across the city, and it doesn't matter anymore whose they are. It was one friend's wedding anniversary. Another friend was on the subway when it happened, going to Brooklyn, and was probably underneath the World Trade Center moments before it was hit, although she didn't find out until halfway through the class she went on to teach. Someone else, working in midtown, heard when her mother called her office from Turkey, checking that she was alive. An acquaintance was, like many of my colleagues in the New York film community, in Toronto for the film festival there. He found out by e-mail, in a hotel room, and didn't believe it until he turned on the television. One relative of a friend worked on Wall Street, and was held in his building when the planes hit the towers, not allowed to leave. He looked out of the window and saw people jumping, one after the other, and then too many to count. Eventually he had to turn away. 'It's not like it was on TV', he said.

Rosalind Galt's friends had to tell and share their story because, in the very telling of the story, often again and again, they were beginning to come to terms with what seemed unbelievable. Stories can be crucial psychologically. Nor should their importance politically and socially be underestimated.

Stephen Sykes, a former Bishop of Ely in Cambridgeshire, has said that the British National Health Service owed at least as much to the novels of Charles Dickens and Mrs Gaskell as it did to its founding fathers Lord Beveridge and Aneurin Bevan, because the stories of the novelists showed how dreadful the health and conditions of people were, and how far they were beyond the capacity even of benevolent philanthropy to cope with.

In his 1953 play *The Crucible*, the playwright Arthur Miller told on the New York stage the story of how easy it was in the Massachusetts village of Salem, 300 years earlier, for rumours to start that someone was a witch; and, before long, all sorts of accusations would be flying around and people were being put on trial and executed. Just a story from a corner of American history; but, when the story was told in the year when Senator Joseph McCarthy became chairman of the United States Senate's Committee on Un-American Activities, it became a powerful vehicle in the campaign to prevent the witch-hunt he ran against those he believed were communists.

According to Luke's Gospel (20:9–19), it was one of the stories Jesus told which started the final campaign to get rid of him:

'A man planted a vineyard, and leased it to tenants, and went to another country for a long time. When the season came, he sent a slave to the tenants in order that they might give him his share of the produce of the vineyard; but the tenants beat him and sent him away empty-handed. Next he sent another slave; that one also they beat and insulted and sent away empty-handed. And he sent still a third; this one also they wounded and threw out. Then the owner of the vineyard said: "What shall I do? I will send my beloved son; perhaps they will respect him." But when the tenants saw him, they discussed it among themselves and said: "This is the heir; let us kill him so that the inheritance may be ours." So they threw him out of the vineyard and killed him. What then will the owner of the vineyard do to them? He will come and destroy those tenants and give the vineyard to others.'

Luke then adds that, when the religious leaders heard this parable and realised that the story was about them, they wanted to lay their hands on Jesus and began to look for ways to trap him. But what really made them angry was not just that they were in the story, but that Jesus was putting himself in the story too. 'I will send my beloved son.' The man who told stories became a story himself.

Because we do not always understand how powerful stories are, we are tempted to dismiss stories as vehicles for truth. But sometimes we make the opposite mistake, of believing that the story is a precise description of reality.

Rowan Williams, the Archbishop of Wales, was in Manhattan on September 11th, in a church very close to the Twin Towers. Early the next morning, he was stopped by a man who, it turned out, was an airline pilot and a devout Roman Catholic, and who, recognising the Archbishop's clerical collar, asked 'what the hell God was doing' the previous morning, when the planes were flown into the World Trade Center. Rowan Williams' answer touched on how the world God has made isn't one where he intervenes to prevent dreadful things happening (or where would he stop?) and on how God was present in so much of the sacrificial risks taken for others. But Rowan Williams suspects that for the first time that devout Christian was having to come to terms with the fact that he was committed to a God 'who seems useless in a crisis'.[3]

Ever since the days of Copernicus and the telescope of Galileo in the sixteenth and seventeenth centuries, we have known that the heavens could not be God's residence in space, and since then there have been the measurements by astronomers, the vistas and insights of the satellites, space travel and space probes. But we still cling to a version of the story which pictures God *somewhere*, capable of intervening in this world's affairs. Just as we have to grow out of the idea that God is enthroned in heaven, we have to outgrow the notion that there is nothing God cannot do; and so, once evil terrorists had taken control of the aircraft and were determined to carry out their plan, there was no stopping them – not even by God.

I spent some time in New York in late 2001, making a series of radio programmes called *God at Ground Zero* and talking to various people about how their faith responded to September 11th. One of them was the retired radical Bishop of Newark, New Jersey, Jack Spong. He said to me that, while the religious community ever since then had been trying to answer the same question as Rowan Williams' airline pilot had put to him, it was the wrong question to ask.

> In the first place, it makes an assumption. It assumes that God is a being, supernatural in power, who lives somewhere above the sky – and why didn't God intervene? I don't think that that's the way we can see God – as a being, even vulnerable. We certainly can't see God as a being in judgement up above the sky. We had an American evangelist named Jerry Falwell who said he knew exactly why we'd had

this World Trade disaster – that America has cosied up to feminists, pagans, abortionists and homosexuals in the American Civil Liberties Union. That's the same sort of mentality that we used in the fourteenth century. I think the question that we ought to ask is 'who and 'what' – and I use both words – 'who', because I'm not willing to say that God does not participate in what I understand by person-hood, but I also want 'what' used because I think person-hood is finally too small a category to think about God. God I see as identical with life, identical with love, identical with being, and always emerging in the world – not external to the world, operating on it in some miraculous fashion. Not a God above the sky who invaded the world in a miraculous birth story called the virgin nativity story, nor the God who left this world by the cosmic ascension to get back up to the sky – that's the mythology of the first century. What I want is the experience somehow in some way of this Jesus. People believe that they confronted the very presence of the holy God and it made them holy – it called them into life.

I am not sure Bishop Spong, in his understandable mission to express Christianity in contemporary terms, takes sufficiently seriously a warning contained in advice which one of my old teachers, Professor Alan Galloway, used to give to the 'modernisers' of Christianity: it is the doctrines you want to dismiss to which you must give the greatest respect and pay the closest attention. I am sure he is right, however, to claim that many people who accept unquestioningly modern cosmology take far too literally the theological story which evolved to make sense of a pre-Copernican view of the universe. The bishop went on to tell me:

Christianity was born in the first century in a Jewish world. We live in a twenty-first-century non-Jewish world, a very secular world. The way we think is radically different from the way first-century Jewish people thought, and what has happened is that the God-experience was captured inside the words and the concepts of first-century Jewish people, and we keep trying to literalise these words and concepts and act as if there has been no knowledge revolution over the last 2,000 years. The Bible was written about 1,100 years before Christ and about 135 years after Christ. They thought the earth was flat. They thought the sun rotated around the earth. They thought God lived just above the sky. They thought the stars were God's peepholes so that God could look down and keep God's record books up to date at night. They thought women were the property of men. They thought homosexuals should be put to death. They didn't know anything about germs or viruses – they assumed that sickness was divine punishment. They saw miracle everywhere. They saw miracle and magic all over the place because they didn't know how the world operated. Now I don't mean to condemn that. It's not blameworthy, that's just the way things were in the first century. We don't live in that world. We live in a world where space is infinite, where the idea that God is just above the sky is almost laughable. We live in a world where we know that we weren't created perfect and fell into sin requiring the divine rescue; we were created as a single cell and we merged into life. If there's anything wrong with human beings, it's not that we're fallen sinners, it is that we are incomplete and not yet fully human.

However, one of the problems about Bishop Spong's view is that a great many people do have a very primitive view of cosmology and regard the earth literally as a battle-ground between the forces of good and the forces of evil. The terrorists of September 11th seem to have been among them. The threat to Bishop Spong's twenty-first-century world may come from people with a world view which reflects medieval thinking.

So, we all need to make sure that, when a story makes sense to us, it remains a story and that we resist the temptation to invest the story with either the burden of literal meaning or the sense of descriptive reality. For the important thing about the story is not that it is a factual description, or statement, but a narrative which can draw each of us in. In C. S. Lewis' story *The Lion, the Witch and the Wardrobe*, Aslan the great lion says to one of the four children who have stumbled on his Narnia land: 'I only tell you your own story'. In J. M. Barrie's *Peter Pan*, one of the Lost Boys asks, when he hears he is going to be told a story: 'Am I in this story?'

Stories have the capacity to draw us in, and that is why Jesus believed that his followers were those who are prepared to have their faith teased, questioned, judged, strengthened, broken down, built up and remade by stories they believe they are addressed by. It is also why I believe that, despite all the statements and propositions which theology likes to make about God, we will encounter God more in the story of Jesus' journey from the wilderness of Judaea, where at the start of his ministry he was forced to question what it was all about, to the Garden of Gethsemane, where the night before his death he was still questioning what it was all about. In later chapters, I will be tracing that story and trying to draw connections with September 11th. Meanwhile, however, for many, despite Bishop Jack Spong, the question remains: where was God on September 11th? Since I have suggested that the best Christian answers are expressed in stories, let me express what for me provides the hint of an answer in a story from my visit to New York to make radio programmes.

St Paul's Chapel in Lower Manhattan is the oldest public building in continuous use in New York. It is where George Washington said his prayers the night after he was inaugurated President of the United States; and it was literally in the shadow of the Twin Towers, just a few metres from the World Trade Center. The priest in charge of St Paul's Chapel is the Rev. Lyndon Harris, who told me how he was very despondent as he made his way to St Paul's from his home in Greenwich Village on the morning of September 12th.

I came walking down Broadway, and my heart was beating loudly in my chest, and when I got to about where City Hall is I saw the spire. It was a very moving, a very emotional sight and I couldn't believe the spire was standing. So I came in, turned the key in the lock, and it was such an eerie but peaceful feeling to walk in and see everything intact. It was unbelievable. Not even a pane of glass was broken. I had to get a structural engineer here to make sure that the building was safe, and we began a couple of days later to set up on the sidewalk a concession for the rescue workers, and eventually we started cooking hamburgers and hot dogs out there round the clock. We got shut down by the Department of Health about four times a day, and as soon as they left we would start right up. We were feeding about 2,000 meals a day even then. There have been some significant points along the way. Moving the food stall from the sidewalk on to the porch of the church put us onto a different relationship with the City. I brought someone on board who had his own restaurant so that he knew the Department of Health code, and we could now negotiate that. Then we began hiring massage therapists

and podiatrists and chiropractors, and they have been with us
round the clock since then.

The poet William Blake once said that it was 'here, among
sordid particulars that the eternal design appears'; and perhaps
it was among the sordid particulars of Department of Health
regulations and hiring chiropodists that God was present at
Ground Zero. As soon as the building was pronounced struc-
turally safe, the clergy and people of St Paul's mother church,
Holy Trinity Wall Street, began to provide water and hot dogs
outside, as Lyndon Harris described. An offer was made for
the top chefs of the New York hotels to cook extra food in
their restaurants and send it down to St Paul's. The morning I
was there, breakfast had come from the Waldorf Astoria.
Chiropodists volunteered to care for tired feet, and so a podia-
try clinic was set up in the pew where George Washington had
worshipped. Beds were provided so that firemen, physically
and emotionally exhausted, could snatch a couple of hours'
sleep before resuming their searches. Thousands of pairs of
gloves were donated, and hands which were cut tearing at concrete were protected. Priests were on hand for conversations.
And stories were told and listened to by the thousands of volunteers who flew in to help, and worked twelve-hour shifts
round the clock. That was one way God was present.

I have always liked the idea that Geza Vermez expressed in
the title of his autobiography: *Providential Accidents*. Things
happen, and it is God's way neither to cause nor to prevent them
but to use them. Up until recently, I had thought that the best
example of a providential accident was the story David Jenkins
likes to tell about his decision to agree to become Bishop of
Durham. He went on retreat to Lindisfarne, and after a few days
he still had not made up his mind. He went for a walk and,

coming to a point where two paths meet (very biblical!), he was undecided about which to take. A piece of paper fluttering some distance up one of the paths attracted his attention. He walked towards it and realised it was a playing card, face down on the ground; but, as he bent to pick it up, he already knew which card it was. It was the joker. His mind was made up and his bishop's style was determined. God, I don't think, puts playing cards on paths; but, granted that they are there, he then uses them.

As he showed me round St Paul's Chapel, the Rev. Dr Daniel Matthews said: 'Mayor Giuliani, when he was at the Yankee Stadium, stood up and said: "The miracle is St Paul's is still standing" – and you'll notice at the far end of the graveyard, right across the street from the World Trade Center, there are some sycamore trees, and several of those were knocked down, and we're quite convinced that the impact hit those trees, knocked them down, and prevented the church from being damaged. Not a window was broken – amazing.'

Well, if that's the explanation, then it was the sycamore trees and not God who saved St Paul's Chapel. If Mayor Giuliani's use of the word 'miracle' was any more than an expression of surprise and delight I would be worried, because a God who intervened to save a chapel but not several thousand people would have more than a few awkward questions to answer. However, granted that for whatever structural reasons St Paul's Chapel survived, then by God's grace it became a 'providential accident' in stone. God used it and worked through the visionary compassion of people like Lyndon Harris to use St Paul's Chapel as a very powerful symbol to everyone who visited it.

On the day I visited, the eucharist was celebrated at the altar, but everything else continued: in the side aisle men slept, and sausages and scrambled eggs were being served at the back of the church, and in George Washington's pew feet were being washed, and on walkie-talkies (with the volume turned down reverentially low) contact continued between the respite volunteers in the chapel and the rescuers still with work to do at Ground Zero. And the priest spoke the words of institution. 'This is my body. This is my blood.'

A liturgy is the words which form and the shape which emerges from them of religious worship, but the word originally comes from the Greek *leitourgeia* which meant the performance of a public duty. What I saw in St Paul's Chapel united the sacrament of the Lord's table (which is recorded in the Gospels of Matthew, Mark and Luke) with St John's sacramental service of the foot-washing in the Upper Room. And it became for me what Iona was for George MacLeod, 'a thin place where only a piece of tissue paper separated the sacred from the secular'.

That symbolises what God was doing at Ground Zero. And there are other powerful connections too. Jesus told a story about sheep and goats (Matthew 25:31–7), which reflects an old Jewish tradition that the suffering of the righteous on earth is matched by the suffering of the Son of Man in heaven:

'When the Son of Man comes in his glory, and all the angels with him, then he will sit on the throne of his glory. All the nations will be gathered before him, and he will separate people one from another as a shepherd separates the sheep from the goats, and he will put the sheep at his right hand and the goats at the left. Then the king will say to those at his right hand: "Come you that are blessed by my Father, inherit the kingdom prepared for you from the foundation of the world; for I was hungry and you gave me food; I was thirsty and you gave me something to drink; I was a stranger and you welcomed me; I was naked and you gave me

clothing; I was sick and you took care of me; I was in prison
and you visited me." Then the righteous will answer him:
"Lord, when was it that we saw you hungry and gave you
food, or thirsty and gave you something to drink? And when
was it that we saw you a stranger and welcomed you, or
naked and gave you clothing? And when was it that we saw
you sick or in prison and visited you?" And the king will
answer them: "Truly I tell you, just as you did it to one of
the least of these who are members of my family, you did it
to me".'

Across the Brooklyn Bridge from Manhattan, the Red Cross set
up a centre as a base for all the volunteers who wanted to help
at Ground Zero. One of them I spoke to was Cherie Fost, who
lived with her husband on a military base in Iceland but knew,
as soon as she heard what had happened on September 11th,
that her place was with the rescue workers at Ground Zero,
because she had committed herself to be called to action
whenever and wherever the Red Cross needed her. She hitched
a lift from Iceland to New York on the only plane available. It
was Air Force 2, normally the transport for the Vice-President.
'In the first few years I worked with the Red Cross,' she told
me, 'I think the toll was a lot. I can remember being physically
exhausted for a good chunk of the first five years. But I'll freely
admit that this has been much harder than any of the rest for me.
I've been here since September 12th and we've been running
twenty-four hours a day pretty hard for most of that time. But I
have a real connection to a belief that we are all our brother's
keeper, so I think sometimes we do things and push a little
harder.'

For most people, one of the most powerful and moving stories
to emerge from Ground Zero was of the chaplain to the New

York Fire Brigade who died when struck by masonry as he made his way into the wreckage of the Twin Towers to comfort and give the last rites to the firemen who had themselves given their lives by going back into the crumbling building. The pictures of firemen carrying first his body from the wreckage and then his coffin through the streets of New York was one of the most moving icons of twenty-first-century faith.

When did we see you in need, Lord?

So, perhaps if we ask where God was at Ground Zero, we should recall that story Jesus told about the anonymous Saviour who is given food, and remember in the aftermath of September 11th those who were hungry for news of relatives and friends and were comforted by strangers who just came to help, or the owners of cafes and stalls who unwittingly met the needs of one who said he was thirsty and was given something to drink, and provided water or tea or coffee for those dry and parched from the dust and rubble, or the passers-by who spoke quietly to the bereaved who held up up a photograph of their loved one and who became for these mourning people the strangers who welcomed them.

In the aftermath of Ground Zero, God was in Christ in the stranger's guise, naked and being clothed through the funds that were raised and the collections that were gathered to provide for widows and orphans, widowers and children; or sick and being visited as hospitals were inundated with help not just from New York but from all round the world; or encountered in prison as, often with their bare hands and through long, long nights of frustration and despair, rescue workers fought to try to release anyone trapped under the concrete.

# 2

# Hope in Hopeless Hell?

AROUND the world, as we watched on television the flames explode out of the World Trade Center, it was not at all difficult to understand why hell is so often pictured as a place of relentless fire. We tried to imagine the fear of those trapped, which was expressed so vividly in the pictures of many of them preferring to die jumping from a height from which survival was impossible rather than be consumed by the flames. When I visited Ground Zero exactly two months after the attack on the Twin Towers, I could still see fires breaking out as more rubble was removed, allowing air to ignite buried smouldering ashes. Our recordings were frequently accompanied by the sound of hoses dousing another fire. I have no sense of smell, but my colleagues described to me very vividly the acrid stench of burning which penetrated several blocks into Manhattan.

More than once at the time and even more so afterwards, September 11th was described as 'hell'. At St Paul's Chapel, Father Lyndon Harris told me that, two days after September 11th, 'I was working in the morgue, doing last rites, really, on body bags, and I'll never forget this group of firemen coming out of the site, covered in ashes, but weeping, because they were trying their best to find one of the firemen's two brothers (one brother was a fireman and the other was a policeman), and they had been digging for hours and hours and hours, frantically searching for this brother'. And the co-ordinator of the volunteers at the Chapel, Katherine Avery, also described meeting

firemen who came into the Chapel for respite after pulling out
the bodies of their friends.

New York City set up a family assistance and disaster
assistance centre in one of the Hudson River piers. The spiritual
care co-ordinator there, a Roman Catholic priest named Father
John Hutchison Hall, told me that in the two months between
September 11th and my visit, he and his colleagues had coun-
selled 40,000 people traumatised through loss of family, friends,
home or job, and they were still seeing around 500 people a
day. These are the bald statistics of the hellish suffering which
reverberated from the crash of the Twin Towers. On the day I
arrived in New York, a newspaper reported that the New York
Fire Chief, Thomas von Essen, was expected to be leaving his
post shortly because he was 'emotionally spent' attending three
or four funerals a day.

If you want to find out why hell and fire were linked together,
you need to go to a much older city than New York: to the city
of Jerusalem. Between the rocky hill where the Scots Kirk
stands, with its distinctive tower visible from all around and
the St Andrew's Cross always flying proudly from the top of
the tower, and the south wall of the old city of Jerusalem, there
is a valley. It is called the Valley of Hinnom. There in Old
Testament times, people had sacrificed their children to the
pagan god Moloch. To put a stop to any more child sacrifices,
the valley was used as the city's rubbish dump, and the corpses
of criminals or paupers, who weren't buried in family graves,
were thrown into the Valley of Hinnom too; and to keep reducing
the city's rubble and the human remains, a kind of everlasting
bonfire was kept lit. If the body of Jesus of Nazareth had not
been buried in Joseph of Arimathaea's hollow rock, it would
more than likely have been thrown into the Valley of Hinnom.

From the earliest days of their religion, Jewish people had

imagined that the souls of the dead went to a gloomy under-world called Sheol. Later, after they had been in exile in Babylon and returned to Jerusalem, the belief grew that Sheol, for all its gloominess, was too good for those who had been wicked, and so they imagined a fate like the Valley of Hinnom, with its permanent smouldering flames. Sometimes the Valley of Hinnom was known by another name, Gehenna; but the idea behind the names was to make a comparison. The fate of the wicked was *likened* to Gehenna or Hinnom. There was no suggestion that the wicked would live in endless torture from the fires which destroyed or the worms which consumed. It was a picture – but no more than a picture.

The Irish poet Brendan Kennelly defines hell in one of his poems as 'the familiar stripped of all wonder'. In his long poem 'Judas', he confesses:

I can betray a god because I never heard a girl sing
Or steps in the street or sunlight blessing a field of corn.[4]

Brendan Kennelly's poem is about Judas Iscariot, and some years ago he recorded a programme with me for Good Friday. He said then that when he started work on this long poem, he always referred to Judas in the third person. Judas did this or that. However, as time went on, imperceptibly he found himself using the first person ('I kiss the tired legends in his eyes').

Some time ago in London there was an exhibition of paintings grouped together under the title 'The Genius of Rome'. One of the paintings was called 'The Arrest in the Garden' by the sixteenth-century Italian artist Caravaggio, and it depicts what happened later on Maundy Thursday in the Garden of Gethsemane. There, in the picture, were the soldiers and some disciples and Judas about to kiss Jesus. As is usual with

Caravaggio, the scene was lit by light streaming in from an outside source, beyond the picture's frame. But, unusually for Caravaggio, the scene is also lit from within the painting, by a young man, holding a lantern above the heads of the soldiers and the disciples, illuminating the encounter between Judas and Jesus The young man is Caravaggio himself, as if to say that if we want to shed light on what happened in Gethsemane, then some of that light will come from what we ourselves bring to the event, as we see ourselves as part of that story.

Some years ago, a friend whose family came from East Germany showed me round Berlin. On a wet Sunday afternoon, he took me to a square near the centre of the city. On the ground, in the middle of the cobbled square, was a plaque which said that this memorial commemorated the time in the early 1930s when the Nazis confiscated the books of all the authors of whom they disapproved, and impounded the books of all the teachers who had opposed them, and on this spot burned them. There, at my feet, was a piece of glass about a metre square. It seemed a strange memorial. I leaned over it and looked down, but I could see nothing. Gingerly, I put my foot on the brass round the edge and looked down, but I could see nothing. My friend then said: 'Go on. Just stand on it.' And when I stood on the glass and looked down, I saw below me rows and rows of empty bookshelves. And beside them, my own reflection.

The story of the burning of the books and the causing of the empty bookshelves was long ago. It wasn't even a story from my country. But I wasn't allowed to be a detached observer, or a casual spectator. The reflection said to me that I was involved in this story, whether I liked it or not.

Whenever we think of Judas as somebody else, or of evil as somewhere 'out there' in the distance separate from ourselves, we make a serious mistake. A wise man once said that the line between good and evil does not run between people, it runs through people. So Judas is not somebody else. Judas is the shadowy part of myself that I do not want to face up to. Judas is the dark side of myself that I am loath to acknowledge. And every time I hurl criticism at the people I condemn, every time I pass judgement on people whose actions I dislike, and every time I damn those I think have done wrong, I am avoiding the dark side of myself, and running away from the part of me that might have been there with the condemned, with the traitor, with the damned . . . but for the grace of God.

When, immediately after September 11th, some of America's conservative religious leaders explained the atrocity as divine retribution for the country's acquiescence in a liberal agenda, they were indulging in a destructive search for someone to blame – destructive because looking for someone to blame allows us to avoid facing up to any responsibility we might have. Perhaps Judas Iscariot was demonised in Christian faith's early years precisely for that reason.

It is quite possible that Judas himself has been the victim of our perennial need to find someone to blame when, perhaps, the real picture of Judas is very different.

The scholar William Klassen[5] has made a study of Judas, and he suggests that perhaps Judas had often heard Jesus criticise the hierarchy in the Temple. But he had also heard Jesus say that when another Jew sins, it is your duty to speak to him directly about it. In Matthew's Gospel (18:15), Jesus puts it like this: 'If your brother sins against you, go and point out the fault when the two of you are alone. If the brother listens to you, you have regained that one. But if you are not listened to, take one or two others along with you so that every word may be confirmed by the evidence of two or three witnesses.' In Luke's Gospel (17:3), Jesus says: 'If another disciple sins, you must rebuke the offender, and if there is repentance, you must forgive'. That is how Jesus himself dealt with Peter, when Peter said that it was wrong for Jesus to suffer and die, and how he treated James and John when they asked for the chief seats in the kingdom. He dealt with the problem head-on, and good relations were restored. How many problems simmer and boil and then erupt because they aren't confronted head-on, with proper humility but firmness? Did Judas want to arrange a meeting, an encounter, so that the criticisms Jesus had of the Temple authorities, and the problems they had with Jesus' attitude, could be resolved? Is that what Jesus was referring to when he said to Judas, at the Last Supper, 'what you must do, go and do quickly'? Maybe *Jesus Christ Superstar* is actually close to the truth when, in the musical, Judas sings:

> Jesus wouldn't mind that I was here with you
> I have no thought at all about my own reward,
> I really didn't come here of my own accord.

A slightly less favourable explanation could be that Judas informed on Jesus to the Temple authorities, though that sounds today worse than it was. We think of 'informers' as 'quislings', people who give evidence against someone on their own side. But Jewish people of the first century thought very differently: every Jewish person was responsible for the life of the whole Jewish people, and so someone could think of themselves as 'a righteous informer'.

What really convinces me to agree with William Klassen that Judas has been unfairly treated is that, for the first 100 years after Jesus' death, the two names most commonly given to young boys in Jewish families who had become Christian were Jesus and Judas. By the second century, the name Jesus hardly ever appears; and only then does the name Judas start to disappear. Even today, in Germany, the law forbids giving the name 'Judas' to a child. Is it likely that, if Judas really had betrayed Jesus in the sense that we have been taught, people who knew Judas and knew Jesus would have allowed their children or their grandchildren to be given the name 'Judas'? If Judas did not betray Jesus, why, when he saw what he had done, did he go out and hang himself? I will return to that question, and try to give an answer which would square with a less harsh view of what Judas did.

I have tried to show how it is possible that we have misunderstood what Judas did, not because I want to exonerate him altogether but because, if his part was indeed a lot less brutal and less of an act of deliberate betrayal than we have believed, it would be consistent with what then was done to Judas' memory and reputation. Judas fulfilled a need that some people have: the need to hate as a way of expressing their love. Slowly, Judas became demonised. You can see that process happening even in the Gospels themselves. When Mark writes the first Gospel, he says that Judas went off to the high priests to hand Jesus over to them, and they were so overjoyed that they gave him thirty pieces of silver. In the Garden of Gethsemane, Judas comes accompanied by the crowd. He gives Jesus a kiss, then Jesus is bound and led away. Almost 100 years later, in John's Gospel, Jesus says that one of his disciples is a devil. It reports that, when Mary at Bethany anoints Jesus, it is Judas who asks why the ointment was not sold and given to the poor, and John adds that Judas said this simply because he wanted more money in the disciples' common funds because as the treasurer he could steal it. In his last great prayer, Jesus says 'not one of them was lost, except the one who must be lost'. By the time of John's Gospel, Judas has been damned for all eternity. And that process of demonisation went on after the Gospels were completed.

It is sometimes a lot less demanding to find enemies of Jesus to hate on his behalf than to take seriously following him in what he said about meekness and humility and making peace. It is sometimes a convenient diversion from the challenges Jesus did present us with, about denying ourselves and taking up our cross and following him to invest those we think are opposed to Jesus with all the wickedness which enables us to hate them instead. It is sometimes a useful distraction from our own failures in discipleship to identify a group within the Christian community who we believe to be opposed to Jesus' teaching. Then we can justify vilifying them.

In some of the reactions to September 11th, I think I heard people's need to find someone first to blame and then to demonise, as when, for example, prominent religious figures claimed that what had happened was divine punishment for America's alleged liberal attitude on moral and social issues. When Judas is somebody else, the heat is taken away from us. I think Judas may have been a convenient scapegoat for the disciples: they could have called what happened to Jesus 'an act of God' – something which was part of God's plan – but that required a lot of very hard explaining. Could the God about whom Jesus told them really have 'done' this to him? If what happened to Jesus was not an 'act of God', then perhaps it was something to which they themselves had all contributed because they had constantly misunderstood Jesus and finally deserted him. With the single exception of Peter drawing a sword in the Garden of Gethsemane, they had not stood by Jesus. They were culpable, but that is a painful explanation if you're a disciple. Judas as scapegoat is a more acceptable one. Over a century ago, black Americans sang:

When you get to heaven
rub poor li'l Judas' head.

They seem to have envisaged Judas at least in heaven. I find it a fascinating question whether it is those who have themselves been treated as scapegoats who are able to release Judas and let the scapegoat in him go free.

Along with our need for someone to hate, and our need for someone to blame, the way Judas has been treated illustrates something else about us. What tend to stick in our memories of people are often the worst things they did. We sometimes define people by the least praiseworthy aspects of their character or their actions. I value the thought that, somewhere in the lost childhood of Judas, Jesus was betrayed because we are usually quick to remember what is shameful and slow to try to find out what might have lain behind it, caused it, explained it or even, perhaps, excused it.

I want now to suggest an answer to the question that I left unanswered: if Judas is not as guilty of betrayal as we've always thought, and if what he did was intended to promote a meeting, a reconciliation between Jesus and the temple guards, *why did he commit suicide?* Was it just because it all went horribly wrong, and Judas could not live with the conse-quences? Well, I'm sure that Judas was unable to live with the consequences of what he did; but what were those conse-quences that drove him to suicide? Matthew's Gospel, which is our source for the story of Judas' suicide, puts it like this: 'When morning came, the chief priests and the elders of the nation all met together to plan the death of Jesus. They *bound him and led him away to hand him over* to Pilate, the Roman governor.' It is at exactly that moment that Judas becomes filled with remorse. Although Matthew implies that it was when Judas saw Jesus was condemned that he set in train the events which led to his suicide, the trial before Pilate had still to take place. The real likelihood, so William Klassen believes, is that Judas was dead before Jesus was even tried by Pilate, far less condemned. So what was it that drove Judas to suicide?

It was one of the most serious crimes known to the Jewish law: for one Jewish person to put another into the power of a gentile ruler, if handing him over might involve a threat to that person's life. What made Judas believe he was damned was when the Jewish authorities, whom he had trusted, handed Jesus over to Pilate; when they, the upholders of Jewish law and tradition, defied their own law and tradition and put Jesus into the hands of Pilate. Perhaps Judas did what he did because he could not live with his part in handing a fellow Jew over to a gentile authority; or perhaps it was an act of despair that those he trusted to keep to the Jewish law and traditions *had betrayed him*. If so, Judas would have understood what Thomas More says to his son-in-law in Robert Bolt's *A Man for all Seasons*, when his son-in-law is telling him that you can set aside the law when you do not like it or it does not support your case: 'This country's planted with laws from coast to coast – man's laws, not God's – and if you cut them down – and you're just the man to do it – do you really think you could stand upright in the winds that would blow then?'

The way the Church has treated Judas is possibly an example of the way we all try to avoid facing up to our part in dreadful events. However, it has been very difficult to suggest that we all have a part to play in the wickedness of September 11th. We instinctively recoil in anger at any such idea, as reaction in Scotland clearly demonstrated.

*The Scotsman* newspaper asked the Moderator of the Church of Scotland's General Assembly, the Right Revd John Miller, to write an article for publication on September 12th. John Miller, a kind, sensitive man, who has been minister in one of Scotland's worst areas of deprivation for over thirty years, condemned the atrocity without reservation. He said that we expect nothing less than that those responsible be tracked down and punished. 'But,' he asked, 'how can the world ensure that what happens next does not simply make matters worse?' John Miller pointed out that

for decades we have seen the developed countries leap ahead. We have used our military might to annexe a disproportionate share of the world's resources, riding rough-shod over the interests and rights of indigenous peoples. More and more people in the rich world, especially in Europe and North America, have enjoyed unparalleled prosperity, and there has seemed no limit to the material improvements which have been within our grasp . . . Many discerning people have feared that the increasing imbalance between the prospering nations and the impoverished would lead inevitably to a violent reaction. Is this not what we have now seen? And ever-more-powerful armaments have now been shown to give no security against such indignation . . . This appalling tragedy, this attack which has detonated massive destruction in the settled pattern of world trade and world travel, presents us with the need to reconstitute our world's systems. Retaliation alone risks further escalation of the conflict between the advantaged and the plundered. Only a complete reconstruction of our world's economic systems can bring hope of justice and peace.

The following day, a former Conservative member of parliament, Gerald Malone, hit back in an article in the same newspaper:

In the wake of America's day of horror – even before the dead were counted – it takes a weird, warped sense of priorities to reach Mr Miller's primary conclusion: 'We need to look at what we have been doing to the world'. The Christian reaction of sympathy with the dead, the dying and their families – which I would count the proper priority for any minister of religion – was brushed over perfunctorily in the rush to make a political point of breathtaking naivety. It turns out the Moderator is a fully paid up member of the 'we're all to blame' brigade that has caused so much recent political damage in those two failed 'peace processes' – the Middle East and Northern Ireland – in which terrorists who abhor peace and do not subscribe to democracy are expected to graciously abandon their weapons for a seat at their enemies' table.

When I read Gerald Malone's article, his reference to the enemies' table made me think of a story in the Hebrew Bible. It is a story about David, who had succeeded his erstwhile patron Saul as king. In the conflict between them, Saul had hunted David down. He had made several attempts on David's life. Eventually David had succeeded to the throne, and if he had been following the invariable custom of the day he would have seen to it that all of Saul's family were eliminated so that any threat they might pose was removed. But one of David's first acts on taking the throne was to enquire if there was anyone left of Saul's household 'to whom I might shew the kindness of God?' (2 Samuel 9:3). In other words, was there anyone of his enemy's family to whom David could demonstrate God's love? And when David is told that one of Saul's grandsons, Mephibosheth, who was lame in both feet, was still alive, David decreed that all of Saul's lands should be restored to

Mephibosheth, and he would permanently eat at King David's royal table.

There is a wide gulf between the way of the world, illustrated by Gerald Malone pouring scorn on attempts to bring potential enemies to your own table, and the way of religion at its best, which sees hospitality, forgiveness and openness as a way of disarming your enemy. Is there anything special, is there anything specific that Christians have to say after September 11th? What sort of language should Christians be talking?

In 1982, at the time of the Falklands conflict, there was a debate in the General Assembly of the Church of Scotland, and in that debate the world-famous theologian Professor Tom Torrance said that whatever the Church had to say must always be able to have been said out of the mouth of the crucified Christ. For the words of the crucified Christ are: 'Father, forgive them for they don't know what they are doing'. It is important for people like Gerald Malone, who accuse the church of naivety about the world and insensitivity to terrorism's victims, to realise that Jesus did not say: 'Father, forgive them and pretend it hasn't happened', or 'Father, forgive them and let them think it doesn't matter', or 'Father, forgive them and let them off with the consequences of what they've done', but: 'Father, forgive them even though what they did was dreadfully evil and they still thought they were justified in doing it'. There is nothing in what Jesus said as they hammered in the nails which says that those who planned and carried out the atrocities of September 11th should not be brought to justice; but, while Christians can rightly share the language of justice, they can never share the language of retaliation.

It does not surprise me when people who operate the levers of power do not want to hear that whoever wishes to be great must be the servant of all, or when people who believe that clout

in the world goes with the big battalions do not want to hear
that the last shall be first and the first last, or when people who
have a fighting mentality do not want to hear that you should
love your enemies. I would be much more worried about the
terminal decline of the Church if all it had to say was an echo
of the way the world works. It was put most powerfully at the
memorial service for the victims of the Lockerbie disaster by a
distinguished predecessor of John Miller's as Moderator of the
Church of Scotland's General Assembly, Professor James Whyte:
'If we move in the way of retaliation, we move right outside
of the fellowship of Christ's suffering, outside of the divine
consolation. There is nothing that way but bitterness, and the
destruction of our own humanity.'[6] So, Christians must be
committed to the language of justice but not to the language of
retaliation.

There is a lovely Jewish legend, that when the children of
Israel escaped from Egypt and crossed the Red Sea, and they
looked back to see the waters engulfing their Egyptian pursuers,
they cheered and cheered. And God said to them: 'why do you
cheer when so many of my children have perished?' We want
God to be the enemy of our enemies, when God won't even be
the enemy of his own enemies. So we instinctively recoil from
any idea that we might be involved in the causes of September
11th because it confuses our neat conviction that our enemies
must be God's enemies too. We also recoil because we cannot
imagine that good, kind-hearted people like us would ever do
anything as horrible. Nor is it simply the case that moderately
well-off people will be naturally tempted to reject Moderator
John Miller's belief that a global economy which allows the
weakest and the poorest to become weaker and poorer is an
economy in which terrorism is likely to breed.

We distance ourselves from the events of September 11th

because they undermine a belief which most of us cherish and will only reluctantly abandon: that goodness, kindness and rational behaviour lie at the heart of everyone's behaviour. We hate to have to admit to ourselves that sensible, rational human behaviour is not in control of the world, that there are incomprehensible forces at work in and through those who planned and carried out the massacres. That is an unavoidable conclusion which we want to avoid. At the time, people said it was like being in the middle of a nightmare; and nightmares develop with a speed and a logic all of their own, which we do not share and cannot understand – that is why they are nightmares.

We hate it when our identity, our picture of ourselves and our surroundings are invaded by an unfamiliar presence or experience which seems to surround us or puzzle us. And, on the global scale, that is what September 11th did to us. All of us, not just the politicians, knew that an enemy had done this, which is the point of a story Jesus told. It is the subject of one of the sixteenth-century artists, Pieter Brueghel – 'Hell Brueghel', they called him, because of the sort of pictures he painted. At first sight, this picture looks like it depicts the comforting story Jesus told about a sower who sowed seed, a lot of which was either wasted or choked by weeds, although what did fall in good ground yielded a great crop. But, in fact, Brueghel's frightening painting is of a much more threatening story that Jesus told (Matthew 13:24–30):

'The Kingdom of Heaven may be compared to someone who sowed good seed in his field, but while everybody was asleep, an enemy came and sowed weeds among the wheat and then went away. So when the plants came up and bore grain, then the weeds appeared as well. And the slaves of the householder came and said to him: "Master, did you not sow good seed in your field? Where, then, did these weeds come from?" He answered: "An enemy has done this". The slaves said to him: "Then, do you want us to go and gather them?" "No, for in gathering the weeds you would uproot the wheat. Let both of them grow together until the harvest; and at harvest time I will tell the reapers, Collect the weeds first and bind them in bundles to be burned, but gather the wheat into my barn."'

The sower in Brueghel's painting is the enemy who has done this. And the farmer in Jesus' story says: 'Let grain and weeds grow together'. The God who was and is at Ground Zero is there, wherever the alien and the menacing, the uncontrolled and the uncontrollable threatens. And, just as we saw that he cannot prevent the evil that threatens, neither can he eradicate it. 'Let both of them grow until the harvest.'

Is it possible to see the horror in a new perspective? The pain and the suffering and the wounds inflicted are the prints of the nails on the hands of the crucified one who battled with the darkness and still lives. He has contained evil, and evil has not contained him.

**3**

# Where there's Death there's Hope

I have my own memory of walking into the BBC's offices in Glasgow around three o'clock on a damp Scottish afternoon, having just spent a couple of hours in the University of Glasgow library reading through the files of the *Glasgow Herald* for the year 1820 as background for a project I was working on. I met a colleague from the newsroom; and, when I casually asked how things were, he told me that there was a crisis because there had been terrorist attacks in New York, Washington and near Pittsburgh, and there might be thousands dead. 'When did this happen?' I asked. 'Just an hour ago', he said as we went our separate ways. I suddenly remembered something I had jotted down in my notebook from one of the 1820 editions of the newspaper. 'Nothing of importance has happened since we last published.' In fact, in the very week the *Glasgow Herald* was reporting that 'nothing of importance has happened', the Congress of the United States declared the traffic in slaves to be piracy, punishable by death! But, in those days, news took a very long time to travel. On September 11th, pictures were beamed round the world as events were occurring, and soon people were telling their stories of what they had seen and how they had first heard about that morning's awful events.

Two different kinds of story emerged from September 11th. There was the kind of story that the Scottish film researcher Rosalind Galt, whose diary I quoted in Chapter 1, was referring to. These are the sort of memories people shared with each other about how first they heard what had happened on the morning of September 11th.

There were, however, other kinds of stories that reflected what people believed was going on behind the events and the different reactions to them. One story which emerged very quickly was that the attacks on the Twin Towers were the product of evil at work in the world. Britain's Prime Minister, echoing President Bush, said in a speech on September 11th: 'Mass terrorism is the new evil in our world today'. The chief of London's police force, Sir John Stevens, described the events in New York as 'evil in its purest form'. The phrase 'the axis of evil' was coined. On the basis of these comments, what was really happening on September 11th was an assault on goodness by evil.

Aaron Hicklin is a British journalist working in New York. Interviewed for a religious television programme in Scotland, he spoke about the destruction of the Twin Towers questioning the very confident story New York had told about itself. He said:

New York was a very positive city, and the Towers more than any other structure epitomised that. They were a symbol of supreme confidence because of their height for a start. They were built in a depression in the 1970s, which is extraordinary. I think only New York, as it had done with the Empire State Building, would build tall at a low time. But more than that, they enshrined the economic buoyance of the city. I think that New Yorkers, maybe not consciously, maybe it is more subconscious than that, saw the Twin Towers as a symbol of the city itself. They epitomised the New York character. They were boastful, they were brash, they were the bigger, better symbol. So when they were gone, that knocked the confidence out of New York. To lose your most confident symbol was something that, certainly in the immediate weeks after September 11th, no-one could quite believe. It definitely changed the way the city perceived itself. Before September 11th, there were lots of divisions and subdivisions. There were people who thought you needed a passport to go into Queens. They had never been there in their lives. After September 11th, only one question mattered: were you here or were you not here on September 11th?

Aaron Hicklin, who clearly loves New York, recognises, however, that the story of September 11th will change and be given a different meaning. 'The story of September 11th is a transitory one. It is there now, but it will change in time. It will mean something else to future generations.'

The stories people have told themselves about the death of Jesus of Nazareth are ones which have changed several times over the centuries. There is a poem by the Orkney poet Edwin Muir called 'The Killing'. It begins:

That was the day they killed the Son of God
On a squat hill-top by Jerusalem . . .

The poem goes on to describe what a passer-by at the time of the crucifixion saw: the scourging, the nailing, three heads turning from time to time, one of them bearing a crown of thorns, and the crowd looking on, indignant or sorry, the women rooted to the spot where they stood. It's the story of the crucifixion which is very familiar from the Gospels. The poem ends:

I was a stranger, could not read these people
Or this outlandish deity. Did a God
Indeed in dying cross my life that day
By chance, he on his road and I on mine?

That poem leaves me with a question. If God is the one who sustains the universe, and keeps it alive, then God can't die. Otherwise, the universe which God sustains and keeps alive would die too. But I believe that when Jesus of Nazareth died on the cross, God did 'indeed in dying cross my life that day'. So how can God, who can't die and still be God, be God and still die? It is a problem which thinking in terms of stories helps me to resolve.

In that poem of Edwin Muir's, there are two stories all mixed up. There is the story of Holy Week, and that story is about what Edwin Muir describes as 'the ceremonial preparation . . . the scourging . . . nailing against the wood'. But there is another story, which begins and ends the poem.

> That was the day they killed the Son of God.
> Did a God
> Indeed in dying cross my life that day?

Two stories: the stories of what happened one week in Jerusalem which we call 'holy', and the story of what was happening on the grand, epic scale.

In the epic story, God in heaven decided to send his Son to save the world. But people refused to respond to the Son's teaching and preaching, and eventually rejected him and put him to death. However, the Son rose from the dead and returned to Heaven to reign there with God for ever. Francis Harold Rowley wrote:

> I will sing the wondrous story
> Of the Christ who died for me,
> How he left the realms of glory
> For the Cross on Calvary.

There is also the story of what happened to Jesus between Palm Sunday and Good Friday; and that is the first story. Samuel Crossman wrote:

Sometimes they strew his way,
And his sweet praises sing;
Resounding all the day hosannas to their king.
Then 'crucify' is all their breath,
And for his death they thirst and cry.

You may recognise this experience. You are in somebody else's house and you are putting the children to bed. No better way to settle them down than to tell them a story, maybe a well-known fairytale bedtime story. So you start off, and you have no sooner set the scene and got into the story than one of the children says: 'That's not right'. What is not right? What is not right is that you are not telling the story in the way they are used to hearing it from their mother or father, with the right details and the right nuances.

Children like their stories to be ever so familiar. So did first-century Christians. Mark's Christians liked the way he told the story, and Matthew's community liked the way he described Holy Week, and Luke's church liked his way of describing the last days of Jesus' life, and John's readers were at home with John's way of interpreting Jesus' death. But, for all the Gospel-writers, and for their readers, behind and beneath the surface there's a battle going on. A battle between good and evil, between God and the devil, between right and wrong. In this epic version of the story, God in heaven sends his Son to redeem the world in about AD 33. His Son is rejected and yet by dying defeats death, then rises from the grave and returns to his Father in heaven.

Why is the story of Jesus in Holy Week the answer to the story of the perennial conflict between light and darkness, good and evil, right and wrong? My three answers are very personal. The two stories, the epic version and the Holy Week story, merge because they are different ways of telling the same story. In the days when the Roman Empire was at its height, they had the notion that perfect manhood was the ultimate ideal. In a sense, they worshipped perfect manhood. So they decided to hold a procession through the streets of Rome and pay homage to perfect manhood. And they found the most handsome man they could and they covered him from head to toe in gold leaf, symbolising the idea. They processed him through the streets, and by the time the procession was over, the perfect man was dead, because covered in gold leaf his skin couldn't breathe.

In my view, the enduring story of the battle between good and evil does not remain at a cosmic or fantasy level where it cannot breathe. The battle between good and evil lives and breathes and dies in Holy Week. It's about the human struggle for power actually crucifying true love. It's about ordinary greed destroying real integrity. It's about typical human betrayal killing absolute trust. It's about all-too-common jealousy wiping out genuine purity. The Holy Week story is about everyday sinfulness at odds with the best of ideals. But do not try to persuade me that true love and real integrity or absolute truth or genuine purity or the best of ideals are will o' the wisps, figments of our imagination, notions which don't actually exist in reality. I see them during Holy Week in the figure of Jesus of Nazareth as he makes his determined moves from Palm Sunday to Good Friday, confronting the human struggle for power in the manoeuvres of Caiaphas the High Priest, facing ordinary temptation as Judas is offered thirty pieces of silver, looking typical betrayal in the eye as Peter denies he has ever met Jesus in his life, meeting common jealousy as a second Herod cannot face a rival for people's affections.

Do not for a moment think that these petty, squalid, everyday things like ambition and greed, betrayal, jealousy are just examples of the way the world works, simply the practical problems of everyday living. In fact, they constantly confront us with what lies at the heart of the universe, what makes life tick: the reality we call God.

Secondly, because they are both expressions of the same truth, the two stories combine. An English scholar of the New Testament, Leslie Houlden, wrote a book about the Gospels called *Backward into Light*,[7] because only once you understand that Easter is God saying 'Yes' to Jesus can you recognise that the two stories have combined. There are the stories about the death of Jesus and his appearances to his disciples, and there is the Easter faith which these stories were written to describe, God saying that Jesus' sort of living is the only life that could be made eternal, the only kind of life and living which could, without any reservations, be the meeting point of time and eternity.

I will have much more to say about Easter in Chapter 6, but my own experience is that every time I have encountered bleakness and blackness, what has happened is not that the bleakness and the blackness have disappeared, but they have been transformed. Something that was bleak has remained. It no longer destroys but enhances life by adding a new perspective. And that, I think, is a little resurrection. Something that was black has continued but no longer engulfs. It adds to my life a new dimension. And that, I think, is resurrection. Moments that have been painful and times that have been hurtful have left their scars; but the scars instead of wounding, in my most honest moments, make me sense the wounds of others. And that, I think, is resurrection, because at these times I come closest to the sort of living and the kind of life that has the quality of eternity about it. In my experience, the two stories combine.

Thirdly, in my hopes, the two stories meet: the story of the conflict between good and evil and the story of Jesus during Holy Week. Think about two defining moments in the Holy Week story.

The first comes in the Garden of Gethsemane, when Judas and the soldiers have found Jesus, and it is clear that he is going to be arrested. One of the disciples draws a sword and cuts off the ear of the high priest's servant. And Jesus tells him immediately: 'Put up your sword. Do you not know that I could call on my Father and he would send twelve legions of angels to my side?' At that moment, Jesus is at his most vulnerable, but even then he will not allow his vulnerability to be defended with violence. One of my hopes for the future, which is difficult to hold on to after September 11th, but hold on to it I still do, is that the world will recognise that the way of violence leads absolutely nowhere, and that even when we are vulnerable, as a nation, perhaps, or as a society, or as individuals, that vulnerability is not worth protecting by violence.

Then comes my second defining moment. Pilate stands in front of the crowd and tells them that because of an ancient custom he can release to them a prisoner, and he gives them a choice. Jesus or Barabbas. And the crowd choose Barabbas. Another of my hopes for the future is that the world will recognise that popular opinion alone leads absolutely nowhere, and that even when the church in its search for a wider appeal, or a government in its appeal for more supporters, tries to convince us that majorities are worth cultivating, they can sometimes be crucifyingly wrong.

So, these two stories, the story of the last days of Jesus' life and the epic story of God wanting to save the world, are both expressions of the same truth, which is why they merge, combine and meet in my mind, experience and hopes. However, as the Christian faith developed, people began to ask: how specifically does the story of Jesus' last days and in particular of his death play a part in God's plan to save the world? They began to tell more stories, now about *how* God saved the world through the death of Jesus. And that led to arguments.

I want to look at several of these stories. Each of them is an explanation of what was happening when Jesus died. Each of them is what theologians call 'a theory of the atonement': what was happening when Jesus died that made a difference to the world? There are different theories about that, but each of them is just a different story which people told in a way that made sense to them. Frances Crosby's revivalist hymn spells out one story:

O perfect redemption, the purchase of blood!
To every believer the promise of God;
The vilest offender who truly believes
That moment from Jesus a pardon receives.

This story says that, once upon a time, human beings were in slavery. We were enslaved by Satan or the slaves of sin. But, in the ancient world, slaves could either buy their freedom or have their freedom bought for them. So God, who wants to free us from slavery, pays the price of our freedom when Jesus dies. In this story, there is a key word: it's the word 'redemption'. Not so long ago, when wages in Britain were low and poverty was widespread, people used to run out of money on a Wednesday or a Thursday, and they would pawn family belongings to get some money to live on until the next pay-day on Friday, when they could 'redeem' their belongings again: buy them back. It's a term that goes back to the world of slavery. When someone was sold into slavery, he or she belonged to the slavemaster; but they could be bought back. They could be redeemed. And all the descriptions of Jesus as a 'redeemer' stem from this story which tells of humanity in slavery to sin or the devil. And we are 'redeemed' through the death of Jesus.

It is not a story which resonates with me; but then, I am not a slave in first- or second-century Rome, born into slavery because my parents were slaves, or captured in battle and made a slave as a punishment for defeat. I have not been sold into slavery in Rome because my parents got into debt and had to sell me into slavery to escape the consequences. If I had known that sort of slavery in Rome, then a story about a God who bought me back from slavery through the death of Jesus would have been a very powerful story for me. Or, if I had been forced to work in slavery on a plantation in South Carolina in the early 1800s, where songs about Moses going 'way down to Egypt's land' to set his people free had a very immediate reference, then a story about the God who bought me back from slavery through the death of Jesus would have struck very loud chords with me.

I made a radio programme with Anne Pettifor, who ran the Jubilee 2000 Campaign which campaigned to have the horrendous burden of debt owed by hungry nations remitted, or *redeemed*. And she told me that the campaign really took off when she was able to persuade some of the churches and a few of the charities that the word 'redemption' was not just a spiritual word. It was a very practical and political word; and, because it was the word which the Hebrew people used to describe how God had 'redeemed' them from slavery in Egypt, it was the right word to use for freedom from a very contemporary form of slavery and indebtedness.

And the point is this: if I had been a slave in Rome or in South Carolina, or a ground worker in Kenya, I would not have asked too many questions about the theology of the story. I wouldn't have asked whether God really made his Son suffer to purchase my redemption – or, if he did, what sort of God that made him? I would just have thanked God for my freedom and redemption, and I would have treasured texts like this one from Matthew's Gospel (20:27): 'Whoever wishes to be great among you must be your servant, and whoever wishes to be first among you must be your slave, just as the Son of Man came not to be served but to serve, and to give his life a ransom for many'. If I had endured the beatings and the torture which slaves had to endure, I would have known what they meant when they applied the words of Isaiah (53:5) to Jesus, the one who redeemed me by suffering as I had suffered: 'He was wounded for our transgressions, crushed for our iniquities; upon him was the punishment that made us whole, and by his bruises we are healed'.

The Sheffield poet James Montgomery's hymn 'Uplifted are the gates of brass' relies on another story told about the death of Jesus.

Uplifted are the gates of brass;
The bars of iron yield;
Behold the King of Glory pass!
The cross hath won the field.

To be honest, it is a bit too triumphalist for me; and when I encounter images of the cross in the battlefield, I immediately think of something Martin Luther said: that when you turn the cross upside down, you make it into a sword with which to pierce instead of the symbol of a body, pierced. But then, I am not living at a time when everyone believed that our lives were

influenced by a war which was going on between the demons
who occupied the space between earth and heaven. I am not
someone who believed I was just a cipher in a cosmic battle that
was going on between good and evil, at the mercy of forces I
couldn't see and didn't understand but which were using me
and everyone else as battle fodder in the war of the worlds.

If I had been someone like that, then a story about a God who
had trampled down all his enemies which now no longer had
any power over me, or were able to treat me as their whim took
them, would have been a story I embraced with enthusiasm. A
story about the God who, through Christ's victory on the cross
over all these demons, had saved me from being the plaything
of these impersonal forces which controlled the universe would
be a very powerful story for me. Martin Luther put it like this:

And were this world all devils o'er
    And watching to devour us,
We lay it not to heart so sore
    Not they can overpower us.
    And let the prince of ill
    Look grim as e'er he will,
    He harms us not a whit;
For why his doom is writ;
A word shall quickly slay him.

Whenever I think that a story about God at war with the
forces of evil belongs to a bygone age, when people believed,
with St Paul, that 'we are fighting not against flesh and blood,
not against human forces, but against the impersonal forces of
the universe, against principalities and powers', then I wonder:
if I had been taught in the seminary at Finkenwalde in Germany
in the 1930s by Dietrich Bonhoeffer, and had watched my

friends join a church which capitulated to all of Adolf Hitler's demands, and if I had seen Jewish friends branded with the Star of David and had found no way to fight the regime which carted them off to concentration camps, would I have been so patronising as to dismiss a story which described human beings in the grip of forces they could not control, or so sure that the future could be trusted to the march of human progress? What I hope is becoming clear is that the story of Jesus' life and death has always been fitted into a much bigger story which matches not only the social fabric of the time but also the needs of the day.

Frances Ridley Havergal's hymn, 'Jesus, Master, whose I am', makes use of language about debts that are owed:

Jesus, Master, wilt thou use
   One who owes thee more than all?
As thou wilt! I would not choose
   Only let me hear thy call.
Jesus, let me always be
In thy service glad and free.

What we owe today is calculated in money: the mortgage payment or the credit-card statement. So we tend to think of the debts we owe in terms of cash. But we would not have thought like that if we had lived in the feudal world of the Middle Ages. That was a very rigid social world: the serf owed duties to the squire, who had obligations to the knight, who had to serve the baron or the lord; and they owed allegiance to the king. So, all the way up the social ladder, people owed the 'service' of which Havergal's verse speaks until, eventually, everything was owed to the king. And if, for any reason, your obligations were not met, then you had to pay 'satisfaction'. The serf who failed to do the appropriate amount of work on the squire's land had to pay satisfaction to the squire. And the squire who didn't provide the requisite number of men to fight alongside the knight had to make satisfaction to the knight. And so, right up the social scale, demands had to be satisfied. To those who lived in that kind of society, it was natural to tell a story in which Jesus Christ made 'satisfaction' to God, the great king of the universe, for the failures and sins of his human brethren.

It is a world far removed from ours; but, if we had lived in that sort of world, it would have made all the difference to us that when life was lived in the rigid structure of the feudal system, when amends had to be made for every duty unfulfilled or for every obligation undischarged, Jesus had met all the demands and discharged all our obligations to God, the overlord of the whole universe.

That leads on to the last of these stories people told about what was going on when Jesus died. It is the rich theme of sacrifice. Of course it goes back to Old Testament times, when animals were sacrificed because the sacrificial lamb carried the punishment for sin instead of you. And this final story sees Jesus as the sacrificial lamb of God who takes away the sin of the world, most graphically expressed in Augustus Toplady's famous hymn, 'Rock of Ages':

Not the labours of my hands
Can fulfil the laws demands;
Could my zeal no respite know,
Could my tears for ever flow,
All for sin could not atone,
Thou must save, and thou alone.

And so, to save us from our sins, Jesus has to be sacrificed. It is the imagery, the picture, which lies behind so many of the great

hymns of Isaac Watts, who seemed to be able to make the language of Old Testament sacrifice his own in a way that few of
us could today.

> Jesus, my great high priest,
> Offered his blood and died;
> My guilty conscience seeks
> No sacrifice beside.
> His powerful blood did once atone
> And now it pleads before the throne.

Least of all does this language speak to me; but, if I had been a
Jewish convert to Christianity, still emotionally tied to thinking
of a God who responds to sacrifices, then it would have been
different. Even religion we have outgrown can still exercise a
powerful influence on us: just ask a friend of mine who still
puts a lot down to what she calls 'Catholic guilt', or a close
friend in the ministry who used to tell me that he found it almost
impossible to throw off the legacy of an Ayrshire gospel hall!
So the legacy of a Jewish past will not have been obliterated
even by Christian baptism. And so, it would have spoken very
powerfully to be told that all the hundreds of sacrifices you
needed to make, not just at every religious festival but at the
important moments in life – when your son was circumcised,
or you were cured of an illness, or there was a marriage – had
now been superseded by what happened to Jesus on the cross.
It would have released you from the constant struggle to keep
up with the sacrificial system, and from the guilt which accompanied failure.

So, some people described what was happening when Jesus
died in stories about the defeat of demons, others as the escape
from slavery, still others as release from obligations, and yet

more as sacrifice from sin. And sometimes, when people took these stories too literally, they began to criticise the stories other people told, as if their story contained the whole truth. But we need to realise that they are stories; and stories, like systems,

> have their day
> They have their day and cease to be;
> They are but broken lights of thee,
> And thou, O Lord, art more than they.
>
> (Tennyson, *In Memoriam*)

# 4

# Hope of Glory?

VERY soon after the events of September 11th, commentators and experts began to explain that those responsible appeared to be driven by the belief that if, in a cause they thought that their God approved, they laid down their own lives, then as a reward for their martyrdom they would immediately enter Paradise. 'He earns himself a place in Paradise', said a man interviewed on television in London about someone from his community who had gone to Afghanistan to fight alongside the Taliban. The crusaders in the Middle Ages believed exactly the same thing about their eternal future if they died inflicting suffering on others. So, however strange, it is a belief that has its place in the Christian tradition: the earliest Christians believed that their martyrs would immediately enter heaven.[8] All others would need to undergo a period of 'purification'. The martyrs were those who had overcome all selfishness. However, this was not thought of as a 'reward'. The martyrs were those who no longer felt it necessary to seek rewards.

The difference between the beliefs of the early Christians and those who committed the atrocities in New York is clear: on September 11th, hijackers sought martyrdom for themselves by bringing pain, suffering and tragedy to others. The early Christian martyrs, unlike the Crusaders, themselves endured pain, suffering and tragedy at the hands of others. There is an even older tradition about martyrs. When, two centuries before Jesus, the family called the Maccabees led a rebellion against the foreign overlords in Israel, they died praying: 'Be merciful to your people, and let our punishment be a satisfaction on their behalf. Make my blood their purification, and take my soul to ransom their souls.' The thinking behind that sort of prayer was that there were people – relatives perhaps, friends maybe, certainly fellow-countrymen of the Maccabees – who were not keeping God's law and so were being punished by God. The martyr willingly took on himself the sufferings of his people and prayed for them as he died. The martyr prayed that his death might be a sacrifice for their sin – and, if the martyr's prayer was answered, God would relax his punishment, and this would give those who were disobeying God a chance to repent.

It seems that some of the beliefs of those responsible for the attack on the Twin Towers come from the same sort of thinking about martyrdom and the same sort of certainty about the rightness of their cause. And there have been references to parts of the Qur'an and the spiritual tradition of Islam which have been seen as encouraging violence towards others, just as you can find passages in the Hebrew Bible and the Christian Scriptures which express opposition to others in similarly hostile terms. All of this makes it necessary for people who revere a sacred text, whatever it may be, to pay attention to advice which the late Tom Allan, a powerful Scottish preacher of the 1950s and 1960s, used to give to people about reading the Bible: always read it in big chunks, or you get it far wrong! There is maybe a hint of a connection, however tenuous, between the beliefs of those who were responsible for the September 11th atrocities and the background beliefs of Jesus of Nazareth. Why did Jesus, against all the warnings of his friends, and despite the hostility of those who were his enemies, steadfastly set his face to go to Jerusalem at a time when he knew he was likely to die? Perhaps he went to Jerusalem because he expected to die; and, in dying, he hoped that the sacrifice of his death, his martyrdom, might give his friends and family, his followers and contemporaries, the time they needed to repent of their sins. Maybe Jesus went to his death believing that he would enable his friends to get to heaven. The difference, of course, between Jesus' martyrdom and the martyrdom claimed by terrorists on September 11th is fundamental. Jesus sacrificed only his own life, and he did so not for himself but for others.

It was put famously in a song which Cecil Frances Alexander wrote for her Sunday-school class:

> He died that we might be forgiven
> He died to make us good
> That we might go at last to heaven
> Saved by his precious blood.

'Do this to remember me', said Jesus at the Last Supper. According to John O'Neill, that meant: 'Do this so that sinners may pray the Father to remember my death for them, and so they may find their way to heaven'.

Until September 11th, it seemed to some of us that America had often been tempted to sanitise death, with its invention of words like 'morticians' and 'thanatologists' and the funeral parlour with the 'deceased' dressed and made up. Evelyn Waugh satirised it so wonderfully in *The Loved Ones*. I remember once being taken by friends in Cleveland, Ohio, to a funeral parlour where a 'reception' was being held for a friend of theirs who had died and whose remains, dressed in his Sunday best, sat propped up in a coffin while we drank iced tea. Afterwards, I expressed the view that my Scottish upbringing had made me uncomfortable with the cosmetic treatment of death. 'What would be different in Scotland?' I was asked. When I described a Scottish cemetery, with eight men lowering a coffin into the earth, probably with wind and rain howling round their ears, my host drove silently on with pursed lips. After September 11th, there could be no pretence, no comfortable cosmetic disguising of death by the embalmers' art. Death on a massive scale was watched, and then played and replayed from the perspective of professional cameramen and amateur videos. And two overwhelming images, impressions, memories remain. They are often to be found where there is death, though seldom have they been globally experienced, making frighteningly real some words of Edgar Allan Poe: 'from a proud tower in the town, Death looks gigantically down'.

The first impression is the sheer obscenity and the profound shock of the moments of the aircraft's impacts and the explosion of flame. There is often an obscenity about death. 'Nothing exists but death; and death should not be', protested Tolstoy. The Spanish philosopher and mystic Miguel de Unamuno wrote: 'Man is perishable. That may be; but let us perish resisting.' It may have been appropriate for a saint like Francis to write:

> And thou, most kind and gentle death,
> Waiting to hush our latest breath,
> Thou leadest home the child of God,
> And Christ our Lord the way hath trod.

In the days of St Francis, death from sword or plague was not always kind or gentle. Most of us, if we are honest, would be more inclined to share Dylan Thomas' protest at death's obscenity: 'Do not go gentle into that good night. Rage, rage!'

Death, however, as well as provoking protest, often inspires admiration at the courage and resolution with which it is faced. And that is the other image which September 11th has left: the determination of so many in the face of impending death, to contact families by mobile phone and express the love that they knew, even then, they would never be able to speak about again. So heart-rending and poignant were they that many of us could not read or listen as yet more accounts of final messages were printed or broadcast. Humankind cannot bear too much reality. But these expressions of affection, love and thanksgiving from on board the doomed planes, and the reports of those who tried, though there was no hope for them, to divert the planes from their targets, touched the world because of the courage they displayed. And they struck that chord which resonated with many, of making it possible, even in such hellish circumstances, to say what you want to say before it is too late for words.

When the wife of the British politician and Lord Chancellor, Lord Hailsham, was killed in a riding accident in Australia, he was devastated. Writing afterwards, he said he found himself agreeing with words written by C. S. Lewis after the death of his wife. 'Talk to me about the truth of religion, and I'll listen gladly. Talk to me about the duty of religion and I'll listen submissively. But don't come talking to me about the consolations of religion or I shall suspect that you don't understand.'[9] There are people whose faith enables them to face death and mourning with trust and resignation.

My times are in thy hand:
Whatever they may be,
Pleasing or painful, dark or bright,
As best may seem to thee.

But there are others, like Hailsham and Lewis, who find no great consolation in their religion.

Richard Holloway, who was to become Bishop of Edinburgh,

fiercely describes a baby's funeral he conducted on a Lanarkshire hillside on a snowy February day when he was a young priest. 'We all stood round the hole and I threw earth onto the whiteness at the bottom and spoke words into the wind. Then we stood round and touched each other the way you have to when there are no words that will do. We got into the black cars, and the doors shut with wistful finality. As we drove back to the city, I was engulfed with the pity of it all. Death should not be. It revolted my conscience. Something was wrong somewhere.'[10]

It is wrong to think that those who can accept death with resignation and trust are people whose faith is strong, while those who find that their faith does not answer their questions are somehow weaker in faith. Acceptance and questioning, trust and anger, contentment and confusion are two sides of faith. You find them side by side in the Book of Psalms. There is the despair of Psalm 88: 'My soul is full of troubles and my life draws near to Sheol. I am reckoned among those who go down to the Pit; I am a man who has no strength, like one forsaken among the dead, like the slain that lie in the grave, like those whom you remember no more, for they are cut off from your hand.' And there is the trust of Psalm 139: 'Whither shall I go from your Spirit? Or whither shall I flee from your presence? If I ascend to heaven, you are there. If I make my bed in Sheol, you are there.' Both are faces of faith and expressions of genuine religion.

Death, they often say, is a mystery; and the word 'mystery' is derived from a Greek word which means to keep one's mouth shut. So, a proper reticence in the face of death is appropriate; and the world's experience of death on September 11th should prompt no easy platitudes. However, whereas we today tend to think of death as the doorway to oblivion, it is possible that

Jesus of Nazareth offers an alternative: the doorway to opportunity. Jesus put it like this long before natural scientists had discovered that in the midst of death we are in life and that without death there is no possibility of life: 'Except a grain of wheat fall into the ground and die . . .'. Everything dies: human, animal and vegetable life all die, as does cosmic life too. The stars and planets have their day; and, if humans do not die, the human race will not change sufficiently for future generations to survive the reasons for previous generations' dying. Life needs death, and where there is death it is always possible that life will grow. It is nature's way. 'Except a grain of wheat fall into the ground and die . . .'. So it is to be whispered rather than shouted, a possibility not a certainty, a hope rather than a conviction, a distant signal rather than an unquestioned truth; but all of these are part of faith, and part of faith's response to the bitter experience of death.

So, now is the time to ask the question: what has the death of one man 2,000 years ago got to do with the deaths of those thousands who perished when the Twin Towers were first attacked and then collapsed? Has one death in Jerusalem any help to give to those trying to come to terms with so many deaths so many centuries later in New York? According to Luke's Gospel (23:33), 'When they came to the place that is called The Skull, they crucified Jesus there with the criminals, one on his right and one on his left'. Jesus' arms outstretched, between two thieves.

Some years ago, BBC Television devised a programme to communicate with an audience which no longer related to the rituals of public worship. It was called *This is the Day*. A former colleague of mine who worked on the programme described *This is the Day* like this:[11] 'Viewers wrote asking others viewing at home to pray for them. Their letters became an icon displayed on the screen, the simplest way of encouraging viewers to worship God in their homes with the TV screen as an aid, rather than watching others through the electronic window. *This is the Day*, broadcast live for more than a decade from home and hospital, generated so much correspondence that the BBC had to recruit specialist staff to answer viewers' letters.'

One morning, I was one of the viewers to *This is the Day*. Someone I cared for deeply had just undergone a serious operation. I had not been given a very hopeful prognosis, and before I went to preach I needed someone to speak to me. So I turned on *This is the Day*, and I found myself increasingly distressed. The letters, 'the icons displayed on the screen', appealed to a God I desperately wanted to believe in, who could and would intervene to cure tumours, but my head kept telling me what I described in Chapter 1, that God cannot intervene arbitrarily to resolve my problems, or where would he stop? On one side of the crucified Jesus, there was a man who would have understood how I felt, for what he expected from someone who had dared to live the life of God was some kind of intervention: 'Are you not the Messiah? Save yourself and us' (Luke 23:39). It is a very natural and very common response to suffering, ours or another's: if there is a God, he will get us out of it. But there is another reaction, equally common, but not just so natural. It is the reaction of people who believe that, whatever the suffering, God must have a purpose for it; whatever the pain, it must be meant to lead us somewhere. This is not a reaction to be lightly dismissed, because I have heard it from people having to cope with far more than I have ever had to cope with in my life. It gives them confidence, trust and hope.

Thomas Becket, in T. S. Eliot's play *Murder in the Cathedral*, puts it like this:

These things had to come to you and you accept them.
. . . This is one moment
But know that another
Shall pierce you with a sudden painful joy
When the figure of God's purpose is made complete.

The other thief, hanging on his cross on the other side of Jesus, would have understood that – for what he expected from someone who dared to live the life of God was some kind of indication that there was a meaning, a purpose to it which would eventually be revealed. 'Jesus,' he says, 'remember me when you come into your kingdom.' And in between there is Jesus, 'pointing as though in either direction', as the poet R. S. Thomas puts it, towards those who want intervention from God that he can act, and towards those who want an indication from God that he has a purpose. Perhaps Jesus is in between, torn two ways: torn between sharing our frustration, anger and resentment that in the midst of suffering there is not the intervention we crave, and so sharing with us those moments when faith provides us with little consolation. 'My God, my God, why have you abandoned me?' Yet Jesus is also pointing us in the other direction, sharing our hope, longing and conviction that there is nothing which can separate us from the love of God; and so, torn limb from limb on the cross, he can say: 'Father, into thy hands I commit my spirit.' So, Jesus hangs in between those who want a God who will intervene and take their suffering away, and those who want an indication that there is a meaning to suffering which will eventually be revealed. Jesus shares these opposite longings because, just as no-one could take the tension between them away from him, so no-one can take that tension away from us.

I have a friend who is fascinated by Russian icons, and he

tells me that, if you look at a Russian icon of the crucifixion, you are only dimly aware that the cross of Jesus is flanked by two other crosses. The presence of the two crucified thieves is hinted at rather than portrayed, because the focus is not on the cross of Jesus but on where that cross is planted in the ground. For, in each Russian icon, as if buried beneath the cross, there is a skull. It is Adam's skull, and the icon reflects the tradition, the legend, the myth that Jesus was crucified on the spot where Adam died – as if to say that the cross heals the separation between man and God that has been there since time began. So, Jesus is crucified not just between two thieves but between his love for God and his love for us.

There was a Scottish theologian in nineteenth-century Scotland called John MacLeod Campbell. He was expelled from the Church's ministry for heresy because he taught that 'God loves everyone with a love, the measure of which is the suffering of his own Son'. The majority of the Church of the time took the view which Robert Burns viciously satirised:

> O Thou wha in the heavens dost dwell!
> Wha, as it pleases best Thysel,
> Send ane to heaven and ten to hell
> A' for thy glory.

John MacLeod Campbell would have none of that. And he described Jesus as being torn apart because Jesus perfectly fulfilled the commandments to love God and love your neighbour. But the two were at odds, and to love two who are estranged from each other is to be torn between loving both yet feeling the agony of their separation. But it is not only Jesus who is torn apart on the cross. We are told that, as he died, 'the curtain of the Temple was torn in two from top to bottom' (Mark 15:38).

The curtain of the Temple was what hid the Holiest of the Holy places from everyone's sight. And the curtain was torn in two. So now we know that God is the sort of God who shares his vulnerability, his suffering, his pain with us. Shared vulnerability is what unites us and God. However, as Dr Daniel Matthews told me in St Paul's Chapel, that is something that American Christianity may have had to learn in the days after September 11th. He said:

We are a people who have turned our theology into a theology of comfort, a theology of self-preservation, a theology of self-interest and individualism; and that theology is not the theology of the Psalter. The 150 Psalms of David contain over and over again the misery of what it is to live, the difficulty of what it is to survive difficult times. And we have so protected ourselves that we almost deny death, much less deny anything like a disaster like this. We have said: 'How could this happen in New York? Everyone else has it happen and we read about it in the *New York Times*, but it shouldn't happen in New York.' Well, it is a new kind of theological awakening that no-one is free of either death or destruction or evil or calamities, and that's the beginning of a different kind of theological structure. And so what we're doing is we're beginning to wrestle now, as a result of this terrible disaster, with 'What is it all about? What is suffering all about? What is pain all about?' – and we've tried to avoid that on our theological journey to seek happiness or comfort or ease or personal satisfaction.

So, according to Dr Matthews, American Christianity has had to find a new story to replace the one it told itself about the God who provided comfort and wealth to those who obeyed him.

However, a member of the vestry of Dr Matthews' church, J. Chester Johnson, has described encountering the lengths people went to in order to deny that they needed a new story. He wrote in *Trinity News*:

> People deal with September 11th in a variety of ways. Some even have a special concoction for denying the gravity and dimension of the horrific event in order to cope more easily. For example, at a business meeting in the Midwest I attended recently, someone postulated that the terrorist attacks weren't really attacks on the United States at all, they were attacks only against the World Trade Center and the Pentagon. I also heard it said in another context that there aren't shrines or memorials for automobile accidents where someone dies or for plane crashes – so there shouldn't be one for the September 11th victims, thereby eliminating the need for any controversy about the future of the World Trade Center site. A simple decision could then be made to use the site for economic development.

It is always very painful to cope with vulnerability. One of the saddest television programmes I ever saw explored the experience of an Anglican priest called James Miller, who was the rector of what appeared to be a reasonably comfortable parish in the south-east of England. He suffered from epilepsy. Three of his parishioners talked to the camera about how, knowing that he was an epileptic, they had tried to make him welcome, to be compassionate, understanding and supportive. But it did not work out because, they said, it became increasingly clear that the rector could not cope on a Sunday. He took blackouts during the service. At first the congregation was embarrassed; then it became critical; then it just stayed away. There was one

Sunday, a member of the congregation said, when the rector dropped the chalice during the communion and the consecrated wine was spilled on the floor. They talked very openly. They were quite obviously good people, who understood why others in the area who did not go to church thought that the office-bearers were cruel and unfeeling for hounding the rector out of his living; but they had the welfare of the congregation to think about. Their dilemma was an illustration of an inescapable truth about the Gospel of Jesus Christ: that it is about weakness, frailty and infirmity, and these are things most of us want to avoid. What the television programme showed was a group of Christian people who were presented every Sunday morning with weakness, frailty and infirmity, and what they were really looking for was strength, an ability to cope, and worship which ran like clockwork. I suppose the congregation would have nodded in agreement if its minister had said that the acceptance of vulnerability (our own and God's) lies at the heart of the Christian Gospel. It was much more painful, and ultimately it was impossible to accept that truth being demonstrated beside them Sunday after Sunday.

When I was in the parish ministry, I found myself faced with a less dramatic version of the same dilemma. The issue of the dismissal of an employee of the kirk session dragged on for months as it waited to be dealt with at an industrial tribunal. People took sides, and the issue was personalised. Everyone, including myself, made mistakes, and eventually one Friday afternoon things reached such a stage that I broke down. I could not face another day of it. The doctor was called, and I was advised to take time off and if possible go away for a while. That evening I asked one of the office-bearers, who knew me very well, to come round to talk so that I could explain to him what had happened and that I needed a break. But all he could say to me was: 'You must be strong for us. You must be strong for us.'

In the story of the last days of Jesus' life, it is the women who are strong; but the Gospel accounts play this down. Alistair Kee has written: 'Again and again the women understood perfectly well what Jesus had taught. Again and again the women showed initiative in seeking Jesus out. It was the women who knew the deep spiritual things, and it was from a woman that the confession of faith came in the most spiritual of Gospels. They were at the cross not because they did not know any better, but because in comparison with the rest of the disciples they did know better.'[12]

Mary the mother of Jesus was there; but then, at least since shortly after the birth of her son, she had known that he would be, in the words of Simeon (Luke 2:35), a sword who would pierce her heart. But, according to the Gospel of Matthew, 'the mother of Zebedee's sons' was at the cross. Those were James and John, who were part of Jesus' inner circle – and they ran away. But their mother was at the cross to the end. That must have been terribly difficult for James and John to handle.

My mother died over ten years ago. She was not old by modern standards, but in the last years of her life she had grown very confused. She had Alzheimer's disease, and for the last few months of her life she was in a church home for the confused elderly. I used to go to see her, and she did not really know who I was. The way I coped when I visited her was by blocking off everything that linked this frail, confused person with the somewhat eccentric but very loving person who used to check my French homework (because she had studied French) and who quizzed me about my girlfriends. I did not want to think of her as she had been, because it was too painful. Like everyone else, I avoid my own vulnerability. The memories I blocked off were good, happy memories. But suppose I had been James or John, aware that my mother had been strong when I had been weak, loyal when I had been frightened, there at the cross when I had run away? It was the mother of James and John who had asked for the chief places in his kingdom for her sons. They would have been expected to fulfil their mother's ambitions for them. How ashamed they must have been, and tempted to block off the memory of what happened just as I blocked off memories of my mother in her younger days. Was that perhaps why they told the story of the events leading up to the death of Jesus in such a way that the disciples' failure is not glossed over but the role of the women was consigned to a walk-on part, on the sidelines, unemphasised and unimportant? So, the medieval teacher Peter Abelard was able to write:

Alone thou goest forth O Lord
In sacrifice to die.

But Jesus was not alone. The women were there, shaming the others, and one of them shaming her sons.

For people of faith, there must always be shame attached to the cross; but there is much more to the death of Jesus than that, and, if the cross only makes us ashamed, then we will become stuck in unproductive guilt. However, if we ignore that element of shame, then we ignore part of what the cross does: it confronts us with our responsibility. It also takes us beyond shame into something much more positive and powerful; but, to coin a phrase, 'shame is the spur'.

When Abraham Lincoln was asked how he was going to treat the southern states who had taken up arms against the Union in the Civil War and had been defeated, he replied: 'I am going to treat them as if they had never been away'. I heard Professor

Willie Barclay often use that as an illustration of what the cross says to errant human beings: 'I will treat them as if they have never been away'. But somehow it does not strike me as saying enough. Yes, God will treat us as if we have never been away; but something which happened at the cross must make us want to come back. And part of that something is shame.

I find that idea very powerfully expressed in something written by Alan Paton, the author of *Cry the Beloved Country*,[13] a book which had such a powerful effect on people in the days of the early awareness of the evils of apartheid. Paton fell in love with a student at the college in Natal where he had taught before he left to run a reformatory in the Transvaal. Her name was Joan, and she was the daughter of friends of Paton's wife Dorrie; and he writes of what happened shortly after he and Jean became lovers.

It was soon after this weekend that Dorrie said to me: 'Are you in love with Joan?' and I said: 'Yes'. She said: 'What are you going to do about it?' and I said: 'Stop it'. She said: 'Surely she must be consulted about it' and I said: 'We have already spoken about it'. Then I said to her: 'I ask only one thing and that is to go down to Natal and say goodbye to her' to which she replied: 'I am willing that you should'. I arranged with the department to take a few weeks' leave, then I drove the four hundred miles to Pietermaritzburg. It was both relief and pain to say goodbye to each other. The day after I had said goodbye to Joan, I drove back the four hundred miles to Johannesburg, subdued and quiet. Dorrie met me at the door of the house, and she took me in her arms in that strange, fierce way she had when she meant something intensely, and held back her head so that I could see the earnestness in her face, and she said to me: 'I am going to make it all up to you'.

So God says to us through the cross: 'I am going to make it all up to you'. But it is my shame, the shame which I find reflected in the shame of James and John, which spurs me to return to the God whose outstretched arms are stretched out not only in suffering but in welcome.

So Jesus was not alone. The women were there: and not just as mourners, observers of the last rites. They were there because the cross is where following Jesus had brought them. And their presence there shames the disciples. But their presence there speaks to me of something else. I know it is a sweeping generalisation, and probably sexist to say so, but I suspect women have a far higher pain threshold than men. Both physically and emotionally.

There's a poem by R. S. Thomas which I find intensely moving. It's called 'Pieta':

Always the same hills
Crowd the horizon.
Remote witnesses
Of the still scene.

And in the foreground
The tall Cross,
Sombre, untenanted,
Aches for the Body
That is back in the cradle
Of a maid's arms.

These women at the cross had counted the cost. They knew the
cost of devotion, and pain, and suffering. They knew the cost
of these things instinctively from the moment they gave birth.
St Paul got it wrong. He talked about a woman's pain in child-
birth being overcome and overwhelmed by the joy of new life
in her arms. But he didn't know about the pain which a mother
experiences mixed with the joy – the fear she feels for the child
to whom she has given birth. And that's a pain that no anaes-
thetic can dull.

Thomas talked glibly about going to Jerusalem and being
prepared to die with Jesus. Peter had talked boastfully about
following Jesus whatever happened. But they didn't know the
cost. Was it inevitable that it was the female followers of Jesus
who instinctively knew the cost of love, and so were prepared
in the end to pay it because they always knew that they might
be expected to pay that price? If you are to follow Jesus right
to the cross, you need to have a very high pain threshold. You
need to be able to bear an awful lot of reality. And of course it
would be foolish to pretend that only women can do that. But
instinctively they know they may have to, and so they symbol-
ise there, at the foot of the cross, the love that knows that it is a
sword which may one day pierce their heart. Mothers often
imagine their children dying, fearing the worst for them, hoping
and praying it won't be so – but, in their darkest and most secret
moments, fearing and imagining. It is not neurotic pessimism,
just maternal realism. So, when a cross is raised on a hillside,
they are somehow prepared, these women.

Ignatius Loyola in a famous prayer said: 'Teach us, good
Lord, to serve thee as thou deservest, to give and not to count
the cost'. I am not sure he got it right. If he meant not to count the
cost too high, then of course he was right. But I picture these
women at the cross as representatives of all who followed Jesus,

who counted the cost well in advance and reckoned just how high it would be, but considered it a cost well worth paying. It is measured in their suffering with Jesus. Most of us are like Peter and Thomas. We blurt out our protestations of loyalty without at all counting the cost we may have to pay. And so we are numbered among the deserters. But those who knew the cost well in advance are there, standing around the foot of the cross, still there, still paying the price.

It is very important to emphasise the presence of the women at the cross because, if we imagine that Jesus faced death alone, we will imagine that everyone who followed him was just like us. And some were not. They were women, as it happens, and they were a lot more brave and a lot more loyal and a lot more true.

The writer Dennis Potter was once on a television programme and in the course of a conversation with the writer Bernard Levin. Potter said that he often thought his idea of Christianity was unlike most people's. 'In what way?' Levin asked. 'People seem to think Christianity is a bandage. I think it is a wound', Potter replied. When I suggested to Bishop Jack Spong that he might prefer to think of God as vulnerable rather than as the distant God of earlier and of others' thought, he immediately rejected the idea as 'pious sentimentality'; but, in my view, the moment he concedes that 'Who?' is one of the appropriate questions to ask of God, and when he says that even if God is more than a person that is one thing to be said about him, he has to acknowledge God's vulnerability. And when he talks movingly about God 'loving wastefully', that is itself an extremely vulnerable thing for God to do.

A God who presents us with his vulnerability is a God we are likely to want to avoid. I mentioned in Chapter 1 that we need a Copernican revolution in the way we think about God.

In the days of Copernicus, society was a hierarchy of power from the lowest peasant who had no power at all, through knights and lords and kings and emperors whose power increased with their importance. So God, it was thought, must hold ultimate power, and nothing can be beyond him. But expecting God to be powerful in the same way as powerful people are powerful is as absurd as trying to measure the amount of water in a flask in inches or the distance between London and New York in grams. The measurement is simply not appropriate.

Dorothy L. Sayers puts it like this in one of her poems, 'The Devil to Pay':

Hard it is, very hard
To travel up the slow and stony road
To Calvary to redeem mankind; far better
To make but one resplendent miracle,
Lean through the cloud, lift the right hand of power
And with a sudden lightning *smite* the world perfect.
Yet this was not God's way, Who had the power
But set it by, choosing the cross, the thorn,
the sorrowful wounds. Something there is perhaps
That power destroys in passing, something supreme,
To whose great value in the eyes of God
That cross, that thorn, and these five wounds bear witness.

The Danish philosopher Søren Kierkegaard liked to express God's vulnerability in a story he told about a king who loved a poor maiden and agonised over how he might convince her that although he was a king he loved her, poor though she was. He considered raising her to the same rank as himself; but that might only convince her of his power to do what he wanted and not of his love for her. He next considered doing what other kings had done and disguising himself as a beggar to win her love for someone of her own station. That, however, would be deception; and true love can never be based on deception. For a long time, he agonised over what he should do. And then he came upon the answer. Thus, the king abdicated.

# 5

# Lord of All Hopefulness

ON the parish website of Trinity Wall Street, *Trinity News*, J. Chester Johnson explained why, many months after September 11th, he still volunteered for the 8.00pm to 8.00am shift at St Paul's Chapel every Saturday night, providing help for the rescue workers. One night, his children Juliet and Gilbert, both adults, joined him on the night shift.

At 2.00am I asked Tom and another volunteer to cover for my children and me briefly, and the three of us alone, after securing clearance from the attending National Guard and the police, ascended the public platform that has been built immediately alongside the Chapel and that looks directly down into Ground Zero. It was a moment we'll not soon forget – the snow gently falling, tall buildings surrounding us boarded and useless, the only sound being the roar of giant machines in the pit under us excavating the remains of September 11th; silent prayers we separately conveyed for the dead – those removed and the dead still remaining, a slight embrace as we together looked down into the burial plot that laid beneath us . . . We walk away Sunday morning from St Paul's, knowing that we will carry memories of the previous hours through the future – and those memories will assist us to come to terms with the grief, the anger, the sadness, and even the mysterious divine love. But I will also carry a more physical reminder as well – a picture, taken by the Rev. Lyndon Harris, the resident priest at St Paul's, from the churchyard of the Chapel – light streaming from the west, and a perfectly symmetrical cross rising from steelwork against a background of unremitting physical destruction that surrounds the undeniable cross, alone so fully dominating the landscape. For years hence, whenever I am distant by mind, heart or location, I will uncover this picture to remind myself of the shrine of St Paul's, standing in the shadow of the cross, shaped so perfectly by severed but abiding beams and girders.

When I read that moving description, I was reminded of two stories. The first was something written 300 years ago by John Bunyan in *The Pilgrim's Progress*:

He ran thus till he came at a place somewhat ascending; and upon that place stood a Cross, and a little below in the bottom a sepulchre. So I saw in my dream, that just as Christian came up with the Cross, his burden loosed from off his shoulders, and fell from off his back; and began to tumble, and so continued to do till it came to the mouth of the sepulchre, where it fell in, and I saw it no more. Then was Christian glad and lightsome, and said with a merry heart, 'He hath given me rest, by his sorrow, and life by his death'. Then he stood still a while, to look and wonder; for it was very surprising to him that the sight of the Cross should thus ease him of his burden.

The other story of which Chester Johnson's description of that steel cross against a mangled background reminded me was a story I heard many years ago in a sermon the rest of which I have long since forgotten. It was about a British diplomat in the middle of the nineteenth century, Sir John Bowring, who was

Governor of Hong Kong, and on one occasion paid a visit to
Macao. The early Portuguese colonists there had erected a
magnificent cathedral on the crest of a hill, but in the sixteenth
century there was a violent typhoon and the cathedral collapsed,
all except the front wall. The cathedral was never rebuilt, but
the west wall remained, with high on the top of it a colossal
bronze cross. Sir John Bowring saw it silhouetted against the
sky, and in his cabin he wrote:

> In the cross of Christ I glory
> Towering o'er the wrecks of time.

It is much loved, that hymn; but its familiarity blunts its
message. How would we handle a version of that expressed in
stark, contemporary realism?

> Jesus' mother watching there
> Close to the electric chair.

The electric chair conjures up in our minds much more crude
images than a now sanitised form of first-century execution.

> The cross! It takes our guilt away.
> It holds the fainting spirit up.

That sounds comforting; but translate it into more contemporary
terms:

> The only sure and certain hope
> streams from that gallows and that hangman's rope.

It is very difficult for us, after twenty centuries of religious
art and reflection, to see the cross as the horrible, gruesome,

torturing thing which in reality it was. Even Martin Luther, when he designed his coat of arms, put roses round the cross to diminish its cruel effect. I have brought the electric chair and the hangman's rope into the picture not in order to obliterate everything except crude, shocking realism, but rather so that the sheer shock (the New Testament word is 'scandal') of what happened on Good Friday can strike us.

The only way we can see what happened on Good Friday is through the writing of the Gospel-writers and through the eyes of a Roman centurion whom the Gospel-writers tell us was an eye-witness to the crucifixion. 'When the centurion who was standing opposite him saw how he died, he said: "Surely this must have been the Son of God".' It has been interpreted as a profound confession of faith. Right from the start of his Gospel, Mark had let us into a secret: that this Jesus was the Son of God. And now the secret is out, the statement made, the reality revealed, the climax reached. And the wonder of it all is that, in the humiliation of the cross, the centurion recognised the evidence of the truth, that the weakness of God is stronger than men: 'Surely this must have been the Son of God'. These words have also been interpreted as a great cry of defeat. Here was this army officer, who had just supervised the execution of someone put to death as a revolutionary, giving the revolutionary the same title as the Romans gave to their Emperor, or as the Greeks gave to a philosopher like Plato. To say of the crucified Jesus: 'Surely this was the Son of God' was tantamount to an admission that Roman justice and Roman law had got it all wrong, and that everything this centurion stood for as a repre-sentative of the Roman government had failed.

Sometimes I wonder whether many of the events of Holy Week have a more natural explanation than we think. Maybe what the centurion said was not intended to be either a profound confession of faith or a great cry of defeat – though in fact it turned out to be both. Maybe what the centurion intended was a simple statement of fact. Crucifixion was an appallingly slow and painful death. Its victims usually hung on their crosses for several days, slowly dying of a combination of dehydration and suffocation. But Mark goes to some pains to point out that for Jesus it was all over in six hours. 'It was nine in the morning when they crucified him . . .', and at three in the afternoon Jesus gave a loud cry: 'My God, why have you forsaken me?' and died. Is it possible that what impressed the centurion was just how quickly it was all over? This centurion, who must have witnessed thousands of these slow, painful deaths which ate into the duty roster because he had to rota soldiers on until the end of each of them came – this centurion, who had seen so many crucifixions, watched this one end in just six hours. Is it possible that what struck the centurion so forcibly was just how quickly it was all over? Is it possible that this is what made him believe that God must have been at work, here, at this cross? If so, then that centurion was like so many who, when they are confronted with something right outside their experience, look for a different explanation.

> Millions, who humble and nameless,
> The straight, hard pathway trod –
> Some call it consecration,
> And others call it God.

So, when you and I find, to our surprise, that where we would naturally expect to encounter despair there is instead faith, and where we would naturally expect to find frustration there is instead hope, and where we would naturally expect to find bitterness there is instead love, we too are forced to ask: surely

God was there? When you and I find, to our surprise, that anger has been met not with more anger but with understanding, or a clenched fist has been met not with a clenched fist in response but with open hands, or when animosity has been met not with returned rancour but with compassion, surely God was there? When you and I find, to our surprise, that suffering does not twist the sufferer, and pain does not destroy the pained, and death doesn't drain the bereaved of all hope, surely God was there?

One of the people I spoke to when I visited New York at the end of 2001 was a very brave woman of faith called Kathleen Flynn. Her son Patrick had been killed in the Lockerbie disaster. She had been a member of Vice-President Gore's commission on airport security which, had its recommendations been heeded, might have prevented the terrorists flying on the planes which wreaked havoc on September 11th. She learned about the attack on the Twin Towers on the car radio when she was travelling for the last treatment in a course of chemotherapy for breast cancer. She is also a very devout Christian. I asked her whether anything said at the time or since by religious people had been of any help to her. She laughed at my question. 'There were a lot of things said that were not a help', she explained. 'A lot of the platitudes that we heard in the beginning, you know: "God doesn't really give you anything that you can't handle" or "There is a reason for this because it must be in God's plan". And you're thinking this is so theologically inept. You don't have a clue.'

When I encounter someone like Kathleen Flynn, who has endured the horrific experience of her son's death at Lockerbie, followed by the failure of the authorities to respond to the proposals about airport security made to prevent a Lockerbie happening again, and who has not become bitter, I sense real faith. She told me: 'Lockerbie was really the wake-up call for America, and the World Trade Center attacks were the real thing. A woman came up to me in church the Sunday after what happened at the World Trade Center, crying, and said: "If only we listened to you, we would not be here".' To meet someone whose suffering has not twisted the sufferer, and whose pain has not destroyed the pained, and where death has not drained the bereaved of all hope: surely God was there? These often ordinary, everyday experiences can be transformed by an extraordinary, unusual faith. These often familiar, conventional experiences can be illuminated by a strange, incomprehensible hope. These often normal, routine experiences can be suddenly charged with unexpected, surprising love. What they mean is that crucifixion is not something we can date and time, or pin down to that moment on a hillside outside Jerusalem 2,000 years ago. Crucifixion is something that you and I will witness time and time again, and experience ourselves time and time again: and the question still is whether God is there, recognised by whoever is at the foot of whatever cross we have had to carry, or by us at the foot of whichever cross we have been spectators at. For those who are fortunate, Good Friday comes round once a year, a day they can mark in the calendar and observe from a distance. But, for everyone some of the time, and for someone at every time, Good Friday is a present experience.

It may seem very ordinary, unexceptional, undramatic, unimportant. Just moments in your life or mine; and we may think there is nothing more to them than that. But the reality is that in these moments there may be a profound confession of faith, because faith is not just a big word to be saved up for the big occasions when big gestures are required. Faith is how we deal with the apparently ordinary struggles and crises and tensions and emergencies of living; and, if what happens is not what people's experience leads them to expect, then they will ask whether God was not there. The reality is that in these moments there may be a great cry of defeat because the victories over evil and suffering are seldom won on the public stage where everyone can see them, but in lives of quiet desperation, when hope occasionally overcomes despair. In those moments, God is there.

Kathleen Flynn's testimony to the faith which helped her through struck me as very important for another reason: she refused to accept the trite assumption that everything which happened must be in accordance with God's will or plan. Neither did Jesus on the cross.

The twelfth-century monk, Peter Abelard, wrote to Heloise whom he loved but lost: 'Put yourself in the position of one of the bystanders on the path of Christ's passion. Are you not moved to tears of remorse by the only-begotten Son of God, who for you and all mankind, in his innocence, was seized, dragged along, blindfolded, mocked, spat upon, crowned with thorns, finally hanged between thieves on the cross?' In the fourteenth century, St Catherine of Sienna said: 'Nails were not enough to hold God-and-Man nailed and fastened to the cross had love not held him there'. More than two centuries after that, the Dean of St Paul's Cathedral, John Donne, who first coined the phrase that 'no man is an island', remembering that the Old Testament said that no-one could look on the face of God and live, wrote:

Who sees God's face, his life itself must die
What a death were it then to see God die?

The nineteenth-century hymn-writer, George Matheson, ended 'O Love that wilt not let me go' with the words:

I lay in dust life's glory dead,
And from the ground there blossoms red
Life that shall endless be.

Explaining what he had written, George Matheson said: 'I took red as the symbol of that sacrificial life which blooms by shedding itself'. There is a contemporary echo of George Matheson's hymn.[14] In 1993, a young black man was murdered in London. His name was Stephen Lawrence. There was an enquiry set up to ascertain whether his death was racially motivated and whether the Metropolitan Police Force had done all that was necessary to investigate the crime. A couple called Mr and Mrs Chirwa had been returning home from a prayer meeting at their local Catholic church. They found Stephen Lawrence lying on the pavement dying. Mr Chirwa felt for his pulse, tried as best he could to stem the flow of blood, and then went to phone the police. Mrs Chirwa, because she believed that the sense of hearing is the last sense to go, cradled Stephen in her arms and kept repeating to him again and again and again: 'You are loved. You are loved. You are loved.' He died, and the police came and the Chirwas went home. Mr Chirwa washed the blood from his hands, and – he said he didn't know why – he felt he should do something with the water and the blood mingled in his basin. So he took it into his garden and poured it on the ground around a rose tree.

And from that ground there blossoms red
Life that shall endless be.

As I walked round parts of Manhattan two months after September 11th, I saw lots of red blossoms, most often placed beside fire stations. One afternoon, I turned a corner from 42nd Street, far away from where the Twin Towers had been, and suddenly came across a shrine made of flowers, letters, pictures and children's toys beside a fire station where most of the crew had lost their lives. On so many of the messages, there was printed in bold letters the date 'September 11th'. I was very struck on March 11th, exactly six months after the attack on the World Trade Center, that America was determined to mark the occasion, because anniversaries are very important to bereaved people. The Scottish poet Douglas Dunn lost his wife to cancer when she was very young, and one of the poems he wrote after her death begins:

Day by nomadic day
our anniversaries go by.

People who are bereaved have the time of a death burned into their memories. A day afterwards, a week afterwards, a year afterwards they find themselves recalling that it was at this moment that death invaded their lives. Perhaps that is why Mark's Gospel is so precise about the time of Jesus' death. At nine o'clock in the morning, they fix Jesus to the cross. At noon, there is darkness over the whole land. At three o'clock in the afternoon, Jesus dies, and at six o'clock in the evening they take him down from the cross. Every three hours, Mark wants us to notice that something happened.

Jan Struther, who wrote the stories on which the wartime film *Mrs Miniver* was based, also wrote the hymn 'Lord of all hopefulness', which is sometimes sung to a tune called 'Miniver':

Lord of all hopefulness, Lord of all joy,
Whose trust, ever childlike, no cares could destroy,
Be there at our waking, and give us we pray,
Your bliss in our hearts, Lord, at the break of the day.

Lord of all eagerness, Lord of all faith,
Whose strong hands were skilled at the plane and the lathe,
Be there at our labours, and give us, we pray,
Your strength in our hearts, Lord, at the noon of the day.

Lord of all kindliness, Lord of all grace,
Your hands swift to welcome, your arms to embrace,
Be there at our homing, and give us, we pray,
Your love in our hearts, Lord, at the eve of the day.

Lord of all gentleness, Lord of all calm,
Whose voice is contentment, whose presence is balm,
Be there at our sleeping, and give us, we pray,
Your peace in our hearts, Lord, at the end of the day.

I find it revealing to compare Jan Struther's timetable of
hopefulness with Mark's Gospel's timetable of Jesus' death. 'It
was nine o'clock in the morning when they crucified him.' *Your
bliss in our hearts, Lord, at the break of the day*? 'When it was
noon, darkness came over the whole land.' *Your strength in our
hearts, Lord, at the noon of the day*? 'At three o'clock, Jesus
cried out with a loud voice: "Eloi, eloi, lema sabachthani?" which
means "My God, my God, why have you forsaken me?"' *Your
love in our hearts, Lord, at the eve of the day*? 'When evening
had come, and since it was the day of Preparation, that is, the
day before the Sabbath, Joseph of Arimathaea, a respected member of the council, who was himself waiting expectantly for the
kingdom of God, went boldly to Pilate and asked for the body
of Jesus.' *Your peace in our hearts, Lord, at the end of the day*?

On a television programme round about the time of the
fiftieth anniversary of VJ Day, a former prisoner in the

infamous camps that built the Burma–Thailand railway was
asked at the end of the interview the inevitable question: had
he forgiven his torturers. It had been a week in which nobody
watching television or listening to the radio could have
escaped hearing one reply or another. The old man had been
fluent about his experiences, but now he paused. 'Well,' he
said in quiet Geordie tones, 'I hope they never do things
like that again. I can't speak for everyone, but for myself I'm
a Christian and I have to forgive.' And he raised his hands,
index fingers pointing high, and left the studio.[15]

That description of a powerful television moment has stuck in
my mind since I read it, not because I can be critical or have any
right to be critical of those who went through unimaginable pain
and torture and have not been able to forgive. I have no right to
be critical of them because there are far, far lesser hurts, far
more trivial slights which I have not only not forgiven but have
not even tried to forgive. The image stuck in my mind precisely
because of how exceptional that old man was, and therefore how
amazing, *how divine* is the love which, as nails are hammered
into the wrists at break of day, can say: 'Father, forgive them'.
George MacLeod once said that 'the historic story of Christ, the
inside story of Christ *suddenly emerges as the inside story of
yourself* – and it's this inner story, this inner parallel that really
makes the Bible inspired, so that to your condition it becomes
the word of God'.[16] That is precisely why, in the Lord's prayer,
the issue of God's forgiveness and our forgivingness are all
mixed up. Forgive us . . . as we forgive. Or why, in the words of
another prayer: 'It is in blessing that we are blessed', we who
have known the cost and the reality of the blessing at daybreak.

'At midday, a darkness fell over the whole land' (Mark 15:33).
Darkness is menacing. Darkness is threatening. Darkness is

frightening, as when you get off a bus on a country road on a
winter's night and suddenly the comfortable familiarity of the
light which had surrounded you is gone, or when you emerge
from a lift and the doors close behind you and you find that the
power has failed for the landing light, and your eyes take time
to adjust and for a while you are disorientated and lost and
things aren't clear. And in the darkness which descends on
Calvary, Jesus is alone, his perception increasingly impaired as
the cross drains his strength, finding it impossible to identify
those around him from whom he might have drawn
strength – the few family and friends who were still with him.
To the loneliness of his pain is added isolation in the darkness.
The one whom Martin Luther called 'the proper man' is alone
in the darkness, but somehow in the darkness Jesus found the
strength to endure it. And it is the experience of others in their
darkness that somehow they have received strength from him.

He came at length
to find a stronger faith his own:
and power was with him in the night
which makes the darkness and the light
and dwells not in the light alone
but in the darkness and the cloud.

And so

He leads us through no darker rooms
Than he has gone before.

(Richard Baxter)

The Gospel-writers say that, when Jesus died, the curtain of
the temple, which divided where ordinary people could worship

from the 'Holy of Holies', was torn in two – and so, we are meant to understand, now we can all see right into the heart of the Eternal. Many of us cannot see God with that clarity, but more in the tentative glimpse which the poet R. S. Thomas describes as an 'almost imperceptible movement of the curtain'. Yet that can be just enough to cope with our darkness: what St John of the Cross called 'the dark night of the soul'.

The darkness lasted till three in the afternoon . . . and Jesus gave a loud cry and died. Your love in our hearts, Lord, at the eve of the day.

I am a great reader of detective thrillers, which of course come in different styles. Those of today are much harsher (their authors would probably say much more realistic to life) than the more gentle treatment (even of violent death) by Agatha Christie or Margery Allingham. But sometimes the older detective writers had a way of recognising the truth. The preacher Eric James describes how, in one of Margery Allingham's books, two detectives are talking about a young thug who is being sought for murder but is being protected and shielded by an elderly aunt. And one of them says to the other: 'I know it: she'll forgive him without question, whatever he has done to her and however high we hang him. It's no use blaming her, she can't help herself. She's only a vehicle. That's disinterested love, chum, a force like nuclear energy. It's absolute.' But the strange thing, the paradox of it all is that, although this disinterested love is a force like nuclear energy, *it is itself powerless*. Love cannot help itself. It has no power to force a response. The moment love tries to manipulate a response, it stops being love and becomes desire. The moment love tries to compel a response, it stops being love and becomes demand. The moment love tries to beg for a response, it stops being love and becomes need.

St John of the Cross, who knew about 'the dark night of the soul', also knew that 'where there is no love, pour love in and you will draw love out'. So, in powerlessness Jesus dies, demonstrating the power of powerlessness:

> And ere his agony was done
> Before the westering sun went down
> Crowning that day with crimson crown
> He knew that he had won.[17]

And so, when evening came, Joseph of Arimathaea came and asked for the body of Jesus. So Joseph bought a linen sheet, took him down from the cross and laid him in a tomb cut out of the rock.

According to John's Gospel, Jesus told his disciples that his parting gift to them was peace; but, if truth be told, the Jesus who walks through the pages of the Gospels does not seem to be a very peaceful person – always on the move, always upsetting people, always asking questions, always restless, unable to settle down, nowhere to lay his head, they said. It may be because we do not really understand what peace is that we imagine Jesus was not peaceful. We think peace is at journey's end; but the restless Jesus knew that peace is a way of journeying. We think peace is a goal to achieve; but the irrepressible Jesus knew that peace is a way of achieving things. We think peace is an answer we are looking for; but the constantly questioning Jesus knew that peace is a way of asking. We think peace is there at the end of all strife; but the perennially searching Jesus knew that peace is a way of striving.

So, the peace he achieves at the last is not out of keeping with the sort of peace he demonstrated all through his life, nor out of keeping with the peace which he promises, just a few days later, to his friends in the upper room. The peace of that tomb cut in the hollow rock is the prelude to the energy of life's risen presence on Sunday morning.

It is not so much a peace as the prelude. It is not the peaceful end to the story but the turbulent beginning of a new story, which unfolds in your life and mine, in the company of the Lord of all hopefulness and eagerness, and kindliness and gentleness, who is crucified and will soon be raised to new hope and fresh eagerness and revived kindliness and refreshed gentleness.

One final word before we leave the cross. In the days, weeks and months after September 11th, Christians and their churches were expected at least to comment on and at most to support the action taken against 'the evil of terrorism'. When I spoke to Bishop Jack Spong, he said to me that 'we saw on September 11th the dark side of other people's superiority religion, you know: "God has called us to destroy the great demon nation of the west. We are in the service of Allah. Our God is the only true God, so we can die for our God and go on to the heavenly regions."'

Because of September 11th, but more importantly because of Good Friday, everything Christianity has to say about its claims must be said in a manner that is consistent with the death of Christ. Christianity cannot speak with aggressiveness about its claims to truth, for there was nothing aggressive about the dying Jesus. Christianity cannot speak with arrogance about its claims to a unique revelation, because Jesus died in abject humility. Christianity cannot compel people to accept its insights, because Jesus came not to compel but to be compelled. Christianity cannot speak with the sort of certainty which permits no questions, because its founder died not with unquestioning certainty on his lips but with that cry of dereliction: 'My God, my God, why have you forsaken me?'

# 6

# The Triumph of Hope over Experience

ENCOUNTERING the death of someone close to you is always traumatic, but many of those who lost partners, relatives or friends in the attack on the Twin Towers had to endure one more agony in addition to the drawn-out public experience of having to share first their fear and then their bereavement with a world which was watching. They had to come to terms not only with their grief but with the knowledge that they would probably never have the chance to bury the body of the one they missed. Funerals are a very important part of bringing bereavement to some kind of closure. The firemen whom the Rev. Lyndon Harris met in the mortuary a couple of days after September 11th were frantically searching for a brother not because they thought he might be alive, nor just because bodies are precious, but because it always makes bereavement much more difficult to handle if we are not able to pay the last offices of respect and love to the earthly remains of someone who has been killed.

According to Mark's Gospel, two days after Jesus died, the women whom a friend of mine likes to describe as 'last at the cross and first at the tomb' made their way to pay their last offices of respect and love to the earthly remains of Jesus of Nazareth. And, in the darkness, they discovered that he was not there. They encountered the truth that Jesus had been promising his friends all through Mark's Gospel, that not even death could tie him down. And Mark's Gospel ends with the women running away in fear: 'and they said nothing to anyone for they were afraid' (Mark 16:8). Some years after Mark's Gospel was written, someone thought that was far too inconclusive a way to end the story of Jesus, so he added a happy ending, with Jesus appearing to Mary and the rest of the disciples, telling them to go and spread the good news. Like bereaved people without a body to mourn, enigmatic endings leave us without conclusions. However, Mark gave no neat, tidy ending to his story, because Mark does not think of Easter Day as the end of the story.

One of the first series of radio programmes I made was called *A Sense of Place*. I asked various people to take me to places which spoke powerfully to them and to describe why these places were important to them. Richard Holloway, who had recently become Bishop of Edinburgh, took me to a cottage below the Ochil Hills in central Scotland, and explained that he had once owned this cottage. It was from here that he and his family had left Scotland for America, when Richard became rector of a church in Boston, Massachusetts. He talked to me about how he believed that moments like that, when we leave one home for another, when we leave a very satisfying job for another, when we say goodbye to friends, are 'little deaths' which in a strange way are foretastes of and preparations for the death that comes to us all.

I think Mark would have understood that, and its sequel: that throughout our lives there are 'little resurrections', anticipating what is to come. You can see that pattern in what Mark tells us of the life of Jesus, moments which one poet describes as 'just like the resurrection': in the wilderness, when Jesus rejects the way of the world, and the way of faith triumphs; at Caesarea Philippi, when Jesus rejects Peter's flattery ('You are the Christ') and seals his own fate ('The Son of Man must suffer'); on the dusty road, when Jesus sets his face to go to Jerusalem; in the Garden of Gethsemane, when, though wanting the cup to pass from him, he nevertheless bows to his Father's will. There are moments which we are able to think of as 'just like the resurrection' because Easter Day is not the happy ending to a sad story. It is the clue you need to understand the whole story.

Mark wants us to grasp a very elusive truth that the joy of Easter is not something which follows suffering: freedom after chains, reunion after separation, peace after turmoil. Easter is the faith which sees God there, present in the chains and the separation and the turmoil, always raising us to life. But seldom do we see it, any more than Jesus' friends could see beyond the bleakness of Gethsemane and the emptiness of Calvary. Look for Easter as the ceasing of the pain, look for it as the grass which is always greener somewhere else, look for it as the pot of gold at the end of the rainbow, and you will miss what is happening all the time.

Two days earlier, these women making their sad way through the half-light to the garden where they had laid him saw the suffering and the evil and the pain which is woven into the pattern of our lives because it is embedded deep in the fabric of the universe. Traditional religious language attributed that to sinful, fallen human beings. When Bishop Jack Spong talked to me about evil embedded in our experience, he used different language but did not minimise how pervasive and corrosive evil is.

When I try to make sense out of the traditional churches' articulations of that God experience, I find them very strange. I find Christianity insulting human nature time after time. We can't gather Christians together in liturgy without telling them what wretched, miserable sinners they are, how there's no health in them, how they're not worthy to gather up the crumbs under the Divine table. This sort of denigration of humanity – now I don't mean to minimise human evil – I think human beings are capable of doing the most grotesque evil to one another. We know that very well after September 11th. But my sense is that that evil comes out of the fact that we're not fully human, not that we are degenerate or fallen or broken creatures. It seems to me that if you look back at evolutionary history, that we've come through a four-and-a-half-billion-year process, and one of the things we've done because of our evolutionary background is that we've made our survival the highest value. We will kill to make ourselves survive, and we will die in the service of our survival. But if survival is the highest value of my life, it means that I'm radically self-centred. I think that's where humanity is.

Do you let the sometimes overwhelming evidence of the world's evil overwhelm you? Do you pretend to yourself that it is not there? Do you run away from it? That is what we are tempted to do; and it is neither surprising nor shameful. However, Easter Day says that there is another way of responding. It is to see that God has always been there in the midst of it, at work through the evil and the suffering and the pain. And, as we have noted before, that is something which Dr Daniel Matthews has seen people having to learn.

Disaster came at a time and in a way that nobody could predict, and Scripture is full of that sort of thing – it's kind of like the first thing you say is: 'Where is God?' Well, God has been involved in it all along, it's just that we've pushed God out of the way and we don't know how to think about God in relation to the disaster until it hits us. You don't change street theology – which is all we have – without saying: 'I'm now

beginning to believe God reigns despite the fact that I'm suffering. Could that be true?' Well, no, most Americans believe
that if God is reigning, then – 'I'm feeling good and happy
and I'm content. And I've got two cars in the garage, my kids
are getting a college education' – that's when God reigns. We
try so hard to avoid suffering and act as if somehow it's
against the nature of God himself. Part of life is death, and
part of life is suffering. The Bible knows that, the Hebrew
Scripture knows that, but our culture has tended to begin to
say: 'We must be able to protect ourselves from hurting.
There must be a pill. There must be a doctor. There must be
a hospital that will protect me from the pain and struggle
and suffering of loving.' Well, there isn't any. And that's the
theological journey we're always on.

I think Mark the Gospel-writer would have recognised that
when someone believes that God reigns despite the fact that he
or she is in the midst of suffering, then that is one of the things
resurrection is about, that it is one of the discoveries the women
made at the tomb. But we will not very often recognise that
this has been going on. There will be nothing like the glorious
certainty that we are mastering our fate or conquering our circumstances. And if we move the focus away from Mark's
Gospel, the first one to be written, to John's Gospel, the last to
be written, we find there too that Easter Day is not about God
appearing as light at the end of the tunnel. It is about God as
the only power who can move us and motivate us through the
tunnel of doubt and sorrow.

John's Gospel (20:1) records: 'Early on the first day of the
week, while it was still dark, Mary Magdalene came to the
tomb'. There is something authentic psychologically about
Mary getting up early in the morning 'while it was still dark'.

Bereavement leaves people unable to sleep well, and that is both understandable and right, for we should not be able to sleep calmly and well when we have just lost someone we love. When sleep does come, it stops the mind whirling; but seldom for long, and we wake, and for the first few moments reality does not dawn, and then it does. I have learned when it has happened to me that there is no point just lying there, allowing the mind to be invaded. It is better to get up and try to do something.

Kathleen Flynn, whose son John Patrick was killed at Lockerbie just three weeks after his twenty-first birthday, which fell on Thanksgiving Day 1988, gave me a very moving illustration of all of this.

> We went to Lockerbie six days after the bombing. I woke up one night in the middle of the night and said: 'I have to go'. And everyone was warning us not to go because of the devastation and the horror, but I'm a visual person and I said to my husband: 'I have to go, Jack', and he said: 'No, I don't think you should'. The word on the street was: 'Tell the families not to come', and I said: 'I have to go. I don't care.' My husband and I went to Lockerbie and we came back on New Year's Day – we only stayed about two or three days – but I had to go.

So Mary gets up, maybe because, like Kathleen, she had to do something; and she got up 'when it was still dark'. John's Gospel never provides details like that without a reason.

I spend a lot of time, and too much money, in bookshops. I very rarely pass a bookshop without going in, if I have got time, and browsing, especially in second-hand bookshops. If you come across a book that intrigues you, how do you decide whether you want to buy it or not? We are well warned not to judge a book by its cover. You can flick through it and get a quick impression of what the book is like. And sometimes I do that. But most of the time we have to rely on what is called 'the blurb'. Either on the back of the cover, or inside the fold of the cover, there is a description of what the book is like; it is a synopsis that gives you enough information to whet your appetite but not enough to give the story away.

You could not flick through a book 2,000 years ago, for books (if that is the right word) were in long scrolls. And you could not exactly unwind a whole scroll, so you had to unwind just as much as your stretched arms could unroll, which means that the opening passages of any first-century book are vitally important. They are *the* blurb. They are not just the opening of the story, the beginning of the book; they are summing the book up, telling you what it is all about, giving you clues that will help you make sense of the book as a whole.

The first fourteen verses of John's Gospel, where John says that light has come into the world and the darkness has never been able to extinguish it, are the blurb, introducing what follows, so that when in the story of Jesus, the Word made flesh, John tells us that it was dark, or it was night, then we should be expecting that underneath what seems to be happening, below the surface of events, a conflict between light and darkness is taking place. There are always two stories going on in John's Gospel. So, when John says that Nicodemus, who thought that all God's work was done and nothing new could be expected, visited Jesus 'by night', or when Judas Iscariot leaves the upper room to meet with the chief priest and his advisers, and John's Gospel adds chillingly: 'It was night', or when, on Easter morning, Mary makes her way to the tomb 'while it was still dark', John believed that the conflict between light and darkness was taking place in all these incidents. Whatever our eyes may tell us, whatever experience may suggest to us, darkness never wins.

Maybe Mary making her way to the garden was an indication that she for one was not going to settle for the darkness, nor accept that bleakness told the whole story. Like a seed germinating under the ground ('Except a grain of wheat fall into the ground and die . . .') and then beginning to push towards where light is, maybe Mary is pushing her way through the darkness in search of light and truth.

When Michelangelo carved four sculptures for the tomb of a pope, he left the figures looking unfinished because he wanted to suggest that the figures were tearing themselves from the stone towards a victory which in no way obliterated the struggle from which they have emerged.

The Easter experience, to be fully grasped, must be grasped by those who have undergone something of the journey towards Calvary. That is something graphically illustrated on Ash Wednesday 2002, at the start of the first Lent since September 11th. Preaching in Trinity Church Wall Street, the Bishop of New York, the Rt Rev. Mark Sisk, said: 'This place, so recently covered in ash, now dispenses ash as a reminder of life triumphant over death'. And one of those who received the ashes, Carlos Yauri, said that because of what had happened on September 11th, the ritual was 'more meaningful'. Of course it was, and not just because of the symbolism of the ashes, but because the significance of the triumph of life over death is most poignantly grasped by those who have known the taste and the smell of death.

However, as well as being most vividly grasped by those who have experienced Calvary, the Easter experience is equally experienced powerfully by those who, like Mary, are prepared

themselves, in the face of the sadness and sourness, the bitterness and the pain of so much that happens to us, to protest
against the darkness and, like Mary, push blindly towards light
and truth.

Move the clock forward a couple of hours. It is light now.
According to John's Gospel, Mary has told Peter and John that
something inexplicable has happened. They have run to the
tomb and found it empty, and, incredibly enough, they have
gone back to their homes. They still have not understood it
yet. And Mary is still standing there, just staring at the tomb. I
have seen that look so often at gravesides: people bereaved just
standing there as if transfixed, gazing with bleak eyes at a
grave. And then someone speaks to Mary. 'Woman, why are
you crying?' And Mary tells whoever has asked this somewhat
insensitive question that they have taken her Lord away and she
has no idea where they have laid him. Jesus says to her: 'Mary'.
Then John adds another of those little pieces of detail which are
loaded with meaning: 'She turned . . .' (John 20:15–16).

It becomes clear after that; but first Mary had to turn round
and look away from what had brought the sadness and distress.
She had to look away from the darkness, and then she saw.
But looking away from the darkness does not mean pretending
that what was dark had never happened, as is made clear by
another moment in John's Gospel when it is night.

It is a week or so later, and Peter and the rest have gone back
to Galilee, and Peter says to the rest: 'I'm going fishing'. We
think of Peter as the one whose denial took place in the courtyard of the high priest's house, when three times he said he had
never met Jesus in his life. But there is another kind of denial,
the kind psychologists refer to when we so bury an experience
that we pretend to ourselves it has not really happened. Perhaps,
when Peter persuaded the rest to go fishing, he was still in that

classic 'denial' stage of bereavement. 'That *night* they caught nothing.' Something else is going on here, John's Gospel wants us to know. Just after daybreak, Jesus stands on the beach, but the disciples do not recognise him. He tells them to cast their nets on the other side of the boat, and when they do they make a huge catch. When they haul it ashore, Jesus has lit a charcoal fire for them.

In one of his earliest books,[18] Archbishop Rowan Williams makes the vital connection.

Some have noted that the 'charcoal fire' burning on the shore echoes the charcoal fire burning in the High Priest's courtyard on another chilly morning, at which Peter warms himself as he denies his Lord. If this is deliberate (and why not? John, or whoever finally edited this episode, does not waste time with merely picturesque details), it is touch of almost Proustian subtlety. Simon has to recognise himself as a betrayer: that is the part of the past that makes him who he is. If he is to be called again, if he can become again a true apostle, the 'Peter' that he is in the purpose of Jesus rather than the Simon who runs back into the cosy obscurity of 'ordinary' life, his failure must be assimilated, lived through again and brought to good and not to destructive issue.

So Rowan Williams, twenty years before September 11th, goes on to say something that we all need to understand after September 11th: that resurrection is about God giving us back our pasts, the pain still there but incorporated in the new reality God makes of us. God gives us back our memories, still with their ability to hurt, but not to destroy. God gives us back our yesterdays, still vivid, but with all the guilt removed. We will all, those painfully and directly involved and those of us

painfully involved but from a distance, move on; and, as Aaron
Hicklin said, September 11th will become something different
to a new generation. So the Gospel moves on from Easter and
its graphic grappling with evil and suffering into different lands
and different themes.

One final story from Ground Zero, which Dr Daniel Matthews
told me.

The President of the United States said to everybody in the
country: 'On Friday' – the disaster was on Tuesday – 'On
Friday at noon, will every church and every synagogue ring
the bell at 12 noon in honour of the dead, in remembrance
of the disaster and offering prayers'. Well, we have bells in
the top of this building, but they're on solenoid so that you
have to have electricity to ring the bells. So you push a little
button and the bell rings. Well, the electricity was all out
because we lost all of our power. So I called one of the
engineers who was down here inspecting the building on a
cellphone, and I said: 'Could you ring the bells?' And he said:
'Oh, Dr Matthews, no way! No way! Because there's no electricity.' Well, about 12.30 my cellphone rang, and he was on
the other end and because he was in the middle of all this noise
and confusion he was yelling at me, he said: 'Dr Matthews,
Dr Matthews, guess what?' I said: 'What?' He said: 'I
climbed up that tower and I found a piece of iron pipe and',
he said, 'I crawled over on top of that bell and beat the hell
out of that bell!' And I said: 'Praise the Lord'. He said: 'Oh,
you haven't heard the best part'. And I said: 'Well, what's the
best part?' He said: 'The best part is when I came down out
of the tower, I got down and all of the rescue workers had
taken their hats off and put them over their hearts while the
bell was ringing as if to say God reigns despite this hell'.

# 7

# Hope Springs Eternal

NOWHERE is it more important to recognise that there are always two stories being told about Jesus than in the account which forms the theme for the first Christian festival after Easter. It is the story of the Ascension as told by Luke (24:50–1): 'Then Jesus led them out as far as Bethany, and lifting up his hands, he blessed them. While he was blessing them, he withdrew from them and was carried up into heaven.'

The First World War poet, G. A. Studdert Kennedy (Woodbine Willie, they called him in the trenches), has a poem which begins:

How far above the things of earth
Is Christ at God's right hand?

If you go into King's College Chapel in Cambridge, on the south wall of the choir there is a stained-glass window which pictures the Ascension. At the bottom of the window, there is a green hillside; and the disciples are there, all of them looking up, towards the arch of the window. And as your eyes follow theirs, in the apex of the window, you see . . . two little feet.

One of my old teachers, a wise Anglican, used to say that he often found considerable difficulty in saying the Apostles' Creed, but he had no difficulty singing it! Maybe that is why we can still sing with confidence rousing hymns reflecting Jesus' ascension:

Crown him with many crowns
The Lamb upon his throne
Hark how the heavenly anthem drowns
All music but its own.

Or:

He sits at God's right hand
Till all his foes submit
And bow to his command
And fall beneath his feet.

If we were to put these sorts of words to the test of rigorous literalism, then we would not sing them, but we do because the language of religion is the language of poetry, and poetry paints pictures. And we should not despise picture language. The writer G. K. Chesterton was once asked to sign his autograph on a child's picture book. After a moment or two's thought, he wrote on the inside cover of the book:

Stand up and keep your childishness
Resist the pedants' screeds and strictures
But don't believe in anything
That can't be told in coloured pictures.

The story of the Ascension of Jesus is a coloured picture, a very brightly coloured picture. But don't dismiss it or despise it because of that. Like every picture, this one tells a story. The Apostles' Creed puts the story in a few short words. It says that Jesus 'ascended into heaven and sitteth on the right hand of God the Father Almighty'.

When the late Professor Willie Barclay, the Scottish scholar whose name is perhaps most known around the world, was given the freedom of his home town of Motherwell, he used to say that being a freeman of Motherwell gave him the right to graze his horse on Motherwell Common! And then he would add: 'which would be all very well if I had a horse or Motherwell had a Common!' And it is tempting for those of a literal mind to hear that Jesus sits at the right hand of God and say that it would be all very well . . . if Jesus could sit or if God had a right hand. But of course, it is a picture too, and it is a fairly primitive picture. It comes from a world which thought of us being here and hell down there and God up in the heavens. And what is being said, in the language of a first-century picture, is that Jesus has gone up into the heavens where he is now and forever part of God. Which means that everything we know about Jesus is true of God.

Do you remember how, in John's Gospel, after Jesus has been going on and on about God the Father, it is Philip who says to him: 'Show us the Father', and Jesus replies quickly: 'He who has seen me has seen the Father'? The Ascension picture says just that: what is true of Jesus is true of God. So, when Jesus welcomes the untouchables and touches the unlovable, the Ascension says that that was God, because what is true of Jesus is true of God. When Jesus forgives the unforgivable, and says of those who are hammering nails into his hands and feet: 'Father, forgive them . . .', the Ascension says that that was God, because what is true of Jesus is true of God. When Jesus mixes with the outcasts and the contemptible in society (and doesn't just mix with them but revels in their company), the Ascension says that that was God. Because what is true of Jesus is true of God. When Jesus says to a few pretty miserable disciples that they will be salt for the earth and light for the world, that was God. So that is the first thing this picture of the

Ascension is putting across: that everything we know of Jesus is true of God.

> The other gods were strong, but Thou wast weak;
> They rode, but Thou didst stumble to a throne.
> But to our wounds only God's wounds can speak,
> And not a God has wounds but Thou alone.[19]

In John's Gospel, Jesus says to his disciples: 'I have conquered the world'. They sound like the words of a King-Emperor, and the Ascension picture is saying that Jesus is the conqueror of the world.

I have become increasingly convinced that we will never really make sense of the Gospels until we stop reading them in little bits. They were meant to be read at one sitting, because the points which the Gospel writers want us to grasp run right through what they wrote. Rowan Williams' comment about the two charcoal fires illustrates that. What Jesus said about having conquered the world is an illustration of that. A few pages earlier in his Gospel, John has told us that, when Jesus entered Jerusalem for the last time, 'the whole world ran after him'. God so loved the world, and it was the world which Jesus says he has conquered which ran after him one day and turned against him the next. Not the sort of world you can colour in on a globe and say he has conquered here but not yet there, but the world of bitterness, and the world of pain and suffering. The world we know only too well. The world where possibilities are always being threatened and visions are seemingly often coming to nothing. The world we know only too well.

'I have conquered the world', Jesus says. Now, we know that no bitterness could grasp him in its vice-like jaws, no pain nor suffering could destroy his faith, and nothing could put an end to the possibilities he foresaw and the visions he shared. 'Rejoice, the Lord is King!' because he has conquered that world which is precisely the world that you and I live in, where bitterness is always trying to get the upper hand, where pain and suffering can threaten to destroy, and where visions evaporate before our very eyes.

Another man named John was to write later to his fellow Christians: 'The victory which overcomes the world is our faith'; and you might say: 'Well, if Christ triumphant has all to do with someone hanging on to hope, and not letting bitterness win, and keeping sight of a vision which is evaporating; if these are the sorts of things which constitute victory, are they not all very personal? Even pious? Is that what the Ascension is all about? What about the resounding claims that the New Testament makes that Jesus Christ is Lord?' That is what the Ascension picture says; too, but it really takes us deep into the heart of another kind of story which we need to spend some time unpacking – the sort of story which the Church has told for 2,000 years in its creed: 'I believe in Jesus Christ, who ascended into heaven and sitteth at the right hand of God'.

A friend of mine, a Roman Catholic priest called John Fitzsimmons, once showed a group of us round St Peter's in Rome. Afterwards, he asked for our impressions. One of the group said: 'It just makes me want to say "I give in"'. And he got the answer from John Fitzsimmons: 'That's exactly what it's meant to do'. What he meant, I think, was that the enormity and the grandeur, the magnificence and the awesomeness of St Peter's in Rome was meant to make ordinary people feel insignificant: pigmies when confronted with the might and the majesty of 'Mother Church'. And certainly not inclined to argue. And sometimes I think that the great creeds of the Church, with their powerful, resounding affirmations of faith, are like St Peter's in Rome. We have nothing quite like them in the faith of the ordinary Christian communities we belong to, whose faith is much more simple and ordinary, just as we are more at home in our local church building than in the grandeur of St Peter's, magnificent though it is.

Like St Peter's, these great creeds are meant to make us say: 'All right, I give in. Who am I to argue with the might and the power of the great, historic expressions of faith? I give in.' The letter to the Philippians says: 'Therefore God highly exalted him [Jesus] and gave him the name that is above every name, so that at the name of Jesus every knee should bend, in heaven and on earth, and under the earth, and every tongue should confess that Jesus Christ is Lord, to the glory of God the Father'. 'Jesus Christ is Lord' was the Church's first Creed. If you wanted to be baptised in the earliest Christian Churches, all you had to be able to say was 'I confess that Jesus Christ is Lord'; but there is apparently more to that simple creed than meets the eye.

Jesus is just a name, of course. I once drove up the steep streets towards the top of the hill overlooking Nazareth, and as we reached the top a school was coming out: children laughing and joking as they made their way into the playground. And someone in the car said: 'Has it occurred to you that this school probably has the most famous former pupil in history?' What did they call the carpenter's son at school? Not Jesus, because that is the Greek version of his name. They called him Jeshua or Joshua. Jeshua Christ is Lord? It sounds strange, but at least that roots the one we call Jesus in the world of first-century Judaism. For Jesus was a Jew, who was born in Palestine, son of a carpenter. And that roots Christianity in a particular person at a particular place at a particular time in history. There was no getting away from it, once you used the word Jesus or Jeshua:

you were rooting your faith in what happened in Palestine at a particular time in history.

Henry Ford famously said 'history is bunk'; and the American poet Carl Sandburg called it 'a bucket of ashes'; but to say that Jesus Christ is Lord is to say that history isn't meaningless, that it does have a point, and that the clue to history lies in this strange, puzzling, ambiguous character we call Jesus, and whom his friends called Jeshua; and that what an English writer calls 'the harmonies of history' are resolved in him.

What does that mean? It means, first of all, that history hinges on this person. Some people say that it is economics which drives history, people wanting money or people needing money – either way, it is money which makes the world go round. There are others who say that it is politics which drive history, and they want to get their hands on the levers of power so that they can dictate the course of events. And there are some people who are convinced that movements drive history. People coming together, united in a common purpose and a common aim. 'There is nothing more powerful', it has been said, 'than an idea whose hour has come.'

But as soon as you use the name 'Jesus', you are saying that what ultimately matters to you and to the world is not anything material like money, nor the sort of ambition which makes politicians tick, nor even the powerful idea which shapes and unites a movement. What matters is this man Jesus.

Today, for most people, the word 'Christ' is just an empty oath; but 2,000 years ago, to say that Jesus, Jeshua was 'the Christ' was to say that he was Messiah. The meaning of this can be approached from two different directions. One you could call 'the Jewish direction', and the second you could call 'the Christian direction'. In the beginning, there was Adam, whose name literally means 'Everyman'; and Adam, according to the Hebrew story, was chosen to represent everyone. But Adam failed. Adam sinned and was banished from paradise. So, next, God chose Israel, his chosen people. Israel – chosen to represent everyone. But very soon, Israel got it into her head that she had been chosen, not just to represent everyone, but because Israel was special. So Adam failed and Israel failed; so God's final plan was to send a Messiah, someone who would represent everyone to God, and God to everyone – and his name was Jesus.

The greatest British religious journalist of our age was Gerald Priestland. He made a radio series called *Priestland's Progress*, and in one of the programmes he said this: 'One morning as I was coming home from my daily contemplative stroll, I found myself saying: "If Jesus was not the son of God, he is now". I cannot believe that Jesus intended his followers to say: "You are the second person of the Trinity" . . . What I do believe is that the company of his followers has come to see God almost exclusively through him, has come to say: "God is like this". God is so like this that, as far as we can tell, God is this. For we are not likely to come much closer.'

When the earliest Christians called Jesus 'Christ', they were not giving him a surname or an honorific title; they were saying that through this particular man, God was at work, speaking uniquely to the world. As I put it earlier, what was true of Jesus was true of God. In Jesus, God was revealing what he was like. That's what it meant to call God 'Christ'. As one scholar put it, 'Jesus is the human face of God'. Or, as a former Archibishop of Canterbury said, 'God is Christlike. And in him there is nothing un-Christlike at all.'

In the BBC archives, I came across a sermon preached by Dr David Steel, when he was Moderator of the Church of

Scotland's General Assembly (1974–5), to the members of Parliament. He told the story of a teacher showing children pictures of animals and birds. One boy immediately recognised a robin. How? The teacher expected the boy to say something about the size of the bird or about the red breast. But instead he just said: 'I ken [know] fine that it's a robin'. That sort of knowledge is not to be despised. How do any of us know that God was in Christ? Why do any of us believe Jesus when John's Gospel makes him say: 'He who has seen me has seen the Father'? We know fine.

The Greek word for 'Lord' is *kurios*. It had a whole range of meanings in Greek. A *kurios* meant not just Lord, but the master of slaves, and the head of a household, and one who had the right to send soldiers to war, and a magistrate who could impose the death penalty. And because each of those was also entitled to be called Lord, *kurios*, this was the title given to the Emperor, the Supreme Power. Christians hijacked the word and used it of the man from Galilee who, for them, was the master of servants, the head of a household, sending his followers to fight, saying that anyone who wanted to follow him had to be prepared to take up his cross.

There is one other word in the English translation of that earliest of creeds: the word 'is'.

Jesus Christ is Lord today.

As that fine songwriter Sydney Carter put it:

Your holy hearsay
is not evidence:
give me the good news
in the present tense.

What happened
nineteen hundred years ago
may not have happened:
how am I to know?

The living truth
is what I long to see:
I cannot lean upon
what used to be.

So shut the Bible up
and show me how
the Christ you talk about
is living now.

# 8

# Spirit of Hope

WHEN looking back to the destruction of the Twin Towers, which, as I quoted earlier, the journalist Aaron Hicklin described as being built to celebrate human achievement and financial superiority, it is difficult not to think of a powerful comparison in the pages of the Hebrew Bible (Genesis 11:1–9) about the tower of Babel, which is introduced to readers with the words: 'Once upon a time'. Of course, we all know what 'once upon a time' means: it means that the story which follows has been made up, like Jack in the Beanstalk or Little Red Riding Hood. 'Once upon a time' means that the story is not true. But what makes a story true? The fact that we can put a time and a date and a place to it? Is that what makes a story true? Is it not, rather, the fact that the story tells us something about ourselves, and about our world, which can't be denied?

'Once upon a time, all the world spoke a single language.' Murdo Ewen Macdonald was one a brilliant group of preachers in Scotland in the 1960s, whose reputation was equally high on both sides of the Atlantic. During the Second World War, he was a prisoner of war in Stalag Luft III, and he was asked to teach his German guards to speak English. One of them, he was quite convinced, wanted to learn English so that he could train to be a spy. So Murdo hit on the idea of teaching him by getting him to learn English from the King James version of the Bible. And so, when this German guard would arrive for his English lesson, he would greet Murdo with the words: 'How art thou, this day?'

And he would be taught the response: 'Verily, this day I am well'. (And Murdo reckoned that he would not last too long as a spy speaking like that!)

The old Hebrew story goes back to a time before humankind was divided by language. 'Once upon a time, all the world spoke a single language.' The story went on to tell how the people of this one world built themselves a tower, with its top in the heavens. And they said to themselves: 'Now we have built ourselves a vantage point from which we can survey the whole world'. But more than that. They said 'Now we have built a name for ourselves too'. And God said to himself when he heard that: 'I will put an end to their arrogance'. And so God caused people to speak many languages, and that brought tension, division and strife. And the great tower began to crumble. And it became known as 'the tower of Babel', because the Lord there made a babble of the language of the world.

It is a story, but it is a true story because it does say something about us, and about our world, which cannot be denied. The story says very simply this: that all our Babels, all our towering achievements crumble to dust when we refuse to accept that we are finite, when we refuse to accept our limitations, when we try to pretend that we are God. Then our achievements bring with them the threat of disaster. That is what the story says: and evidence for its truth lies no further back than September 11th. The evidence, however, has always been there. On the wall of what is now a squash court in the University of Chicago, there is a small plaque which reads: 'Man achieved here the first self-sustaining chain reaction, and thereby initiated the controlled release of nuclear energy'. What an achievement: to get, literally, to the heart of matter. But the chain reaction which that discovery really started led to Hiroshima and the threat which such knowledge still poses. The end of the Cold War has not really diminished it, for there are countries still developing their own frightening offspring of that monster unleashed over fifty years ago. When David Livingstone went into central Africa, it took six months for the news of his discoveries to reach home. Since then, there has been a communications explosion; and the same technology which enables you to speak to someone in Australia as if they were next door enables a Scud missile to be fired off towards a target in the Middle East or terrorists to communicate with each other as they fly their planes towards their targets.

'One by one', says another of the great preachers of the 1960s and 1970s, Colin Morris, 'One by one our towers of Babel crash to the ground when they are prodded by God's finger. Their foundations may be solid; it is their pinnacles that are unstable. Because they are constructed of earthly materials unable to withstand the winds of heaven.' The feast of Pentecost is the feast of the winds of heaven. 'When the Day of Pentecost had fully come, they were all together in one place. And suddenly there was a sound, like a rushing, mighty wind' (Acts 2:1).

Faced with the threats of violence writ large in the destruction of the Twin Towers, or the apparently intractable problem of world poverty and debt, or the danger to the future from the expansion of the countries which possess a nuclear capacity, it is tempting to pull the blankets over our heads and decide there is nothing we can do. And in Britain at least, faced with a Church declining in membership and decreasing in influence, it's tempting to think that too: we are helpless to stem the ebb-tide of the sea of faith. There is not a lot we can do except, just like Peter and James and John and the rest of them, wait for the gale to blow and the spark of faith to be lit again. And we have waited for a long time. But as these disciples waited for the Spirit of God to give them energy and power, they didn't do nothing. Just before the Day of Pentecost, they did one very practical thing. They held an election.

There was a vacancy in the twelve. Judas Iscariot had to be replaced. So there had to be an election. The two candidates were Joseph and Matthias. But there was no voting in this election. The disciples simply prayed, and prayed simply. And then they drew lots. And the lot fell on Matthias. In other words, before the Spirit of God energised and empowered the Church, before the Spirit of God took hold of God's people, God's people had to fill the gaps that were there. And that fits in with the picture that Luke paints of the Day of Pentecost in the Book of Acts, doesn't it? There was a rushing, mighty wind. One of the surest ways to make a sail ineffective is to have holes in it, for then the gale blows through and cannot drive the boat. So the gaps have to be filled. And as well as wind, there was fire. And one of the surest ways to stop a fire taking hold is to create a gap. For then the fire cannot spread. At the first Pentecost, they chose lots, and the lot fell on Matthias.

That says something, today, about the importance of leadership. I once heard about a challenging account of a discussion within the church in occupied Denmark in the 1940s about how it should respond to the German occupation of their land. It was a time when people were advising Christians to be cautious, to say and do nothing which would antagonise.

There is, of course, a proper time for caution. Eberhardt Bethge, the friend and biographer of Dietrich Bonhoeffer, tells of one occasion when the two of them were in a park in the early years of Hitler's power. When Hitler arrived for a rally, there were shouts of 'Heil Hitler!' as people leaped to their feet and gave the Nazi salute. Bethge was amazed to see Bonhoeffer join in and even more amazed when his friend hissed to him to get up and join him. 'This is too trivial for a sacrifice', he said.

No-one could accuse Bonhoeffer of being a coward, and by 1943 his time of caution had long since passed. But in the clergy meeting in Denmark, caution was still being urged. Then one minister reminded the rest that down through the centuries there had been many symbols used for the church, like the lion and the lamb, the fish and the dove, 'but never the chameleon, who takes on the colours of his surroundings'. And he ended his message to the church like this: 'What is our duty? Shall I say faith and hope and love? These are fine words. But I shall rather say "courage". No, that too is not challenging enough to be the whole truth. My dear brothers, in the service of the Lord, our calling today is to recklessness.'

The group of disciples Matthias joined was about to take its courage in its hands and go out into the streets of Jerusalem with the reckless idea that their message was stronger than the forces of opposition which had led them to huddle together in the upper room out of fear. But, before they could go out with that reckless message, they had to fill the gap.

The lot fell on Matthias as a prelude to Pentecost; and that says something too, I think, about the style of membership. There is something very puzzling about the choice of Matthias. He had been one of those who attached himself to Jesus very early on, but Jesus did not choose him to be a disciple. He chose Judas Iscariot instead. Did the other disciples wonder, when the lot eventually fell on Matthias, whether Jesus had been wrong? Suppose he had overlooked Judas and chosen Matthias from the start. Yes, it might have been the sensible decision. But so sensible that there was no Good Friday, no Easter Day, no Pentecost either? God moves in a mysterious way, and the way he works in your life and mine is so often puzzling and confusing and disturbing. He leaves us with so many unan-swered questions. There are so many things we do not know and so many questions we cannot answer. Don't make the mistake of confusing Christian commitment with Christian dogmatism. The Church today cannot afford Christians who think they have got all the slick answers about faith and all the neat solutions to real doubts and justifiable fears and problems which will not be swept under the carpet.

The lot fell on Matthias as a prelude to Pentecost, and that says something about the pattern of discipleship, for we hear not one word more about Matthias. No massive contribution from him is recorded. No significant impact is reported. Matthias just disappears from the pages of the Church's story. But true discipleship is like that. For every Peter and every Paul striding majestically through the pages of the Church's story, there are countless thousands whose names might be Matthias, whose contribution is measured in changed lives and not headlines. But through them the Spirit of God seizes the initiative and works in the world.

Pentecost poses a question. I recently read of how that question was posed pictorially by the artist El Greco. Against a dull background, El Greco paints two women and twelve men. They are obviously extremely excited. Some have thrown their hands in the air, others are craning their necks, others seem in some kind of dream, and each of them is lit from above by a tiny tongue of fire. High in the picture, there is the figure of a dove. There is a thirteenth figure in the painting, not looking upwards but looking outwards at you as you examine the painting, asking, perhaps, what you today make of all of this.

There have always been some in the Church, and they were around in the days of El Greco just as they are around today, who imagine that to be the Pentecost Church you have to try to recapture something of what happened on that first Pentecost: the speaking in tongues, the ecstasy, the strange enthusiasm that seems to have come over them then. But I am not so sure. For did Jesus not say that the Spirit which he would give to his disciples would lead them into all truth, and so the first name which was given to these disciples after Pentecost was 'the people of the Way'? But is it a way that leads backwards, trying to recapture something in the past, trying to rediscover some experience which is locked up in the pages of the New Testament; or is it a way that leads forwards into all the truth that will be revealed? Jesus said: 'When the Spirit of truth comes, he will lead you . . . into all truth'. The road leads on.

The first day of Pentecost saw the birth of the Church, and it is only because the theme of Pentecost forces me to do so that I have introduced the theme of the Church into this book. I do so very reluctantly, because I am always conscious of the warning which the poet T. S. Eliot once gave. He said that the Church was so often like a sign in the window of a baker's shop advertising bread for $1. But when you go into the bakery, there is no bread. All that is for sale is the sign. So, I am reluctant to introduce the Church because we have a Gospel to proclaim and so often we reduce it to a commercial for the Church. In my experience, the Church is often a place where people want to hark back either to a bygone golden age when everything was secure, or else to a bygone way of life when religion was comfortably at the centre, or else to some bygone way of worshipping which kept God and faith securely tied to the past. But, if the Holy Spirit came to consecrate the followers of Jesus as 'people of the Way', then the way leads on.

So often in the Church, it is the opposite which is the case. I remember once, when I was a minister in Glasgow, going to a church in an area which people had left. Where once there had been rows and rows of tenements, packed with families, there were huge gap sites where housing was planned, but far fewer families would live in them. What was the church to do? How was the church to live with the gap sites when they were there and prepare for the new society that would grow round about it?

I talked about the Christian faith being the faith that God was with us on the journey, that Jesus said he was the way and the truth and the life, and the way leads on. And though I say it myself, I thought it was quite a good little talk that might inspire the congregation in this area to move on. Until, that is, one of the elders sitting in the front row fixed me with a glare as steely as the rivets he worked with in the shipyards: 'It's all very well Johnston McKay coming here and talking about Christianity, but it's the future of the church we're here to discuss'.

There is such a discrepancy between all the things we say about the Church, the high-flown claims we make for it, and the reality which many of us experience, a discrepancy which was once described with a reference to the first three words in the King James version of Peter's first sermon on the Day of Pentecost: 'This is that which was spoken of by the prophet Joel'. What the prophet Joel foresaw was nothing less than the great day of the Lord, which would usher in the promised age to come, when God's reign would be everywhere accepted. And Peter says that that golden age is ushered in by this, if truth be told, rather modest effort in evangelism, however much courage it took to make it. In all probability, it was a fairly tiny demonstration of loyalty to a crucified man whom all but a few believed to be dead, buried and done with. The Emperor in Rome was hardly quaking in his shoes. But this moment, says Peter, is that time when the balance of history is being changed. Not just at the start of the Church's story but at the heart of the Church's life, there is always tension and contradiction between the reality and the claim.

The reality of the Church is that we are sometimes blinkered, frequently confused, often quarrelling, occasionally inspired, periodically faithful, usually fearful and not very courageous or reckless people. The claim is, however, that the Church is made up of those whom Jesus described as salt for the earth; and that is a vital role, because in the ancient world salt had two vital functions. First, it stopped food from going bad. Sometimes I think the world we live in can be very patronising towards religion. I hear people ask: where would we be without the wonderful language of the King James version of the Bible or the Book of Common Prayer? Or I listen to people acknowledging that society would collapse without all the good work the churches do; and these are true things to say. But to say that Christians are salt for the earth is to say much more than that they provide a pleasant religious flavour to the cultural world. When Jesus said: 'you are salt for the earth', he meant that we must prevent disintegration, decay and rottenness. You must stop the world going bad, and that means much more than banning the sort of things some Christians disapprove of. It means stopping the world going bad, preventing the disintegration of communities, stopping hope from decaying, making sure that the fabric of faith doesn't decompose, preserving what is good and just and true.

The other function of salt in the ancient world it still has today. Salt makes food more palatable. Very simply, the Church is here to make this world more to God's taste. So much hatred, so much anger, so much violence, so much callousness, so much indifference to human suffering: it must all, so to speak, leave a foul taste in God's mouth, from which, in the old story with which the Book of Genesis begins, God breathes life into the world in the first place. But if the salt has lost its savour? If we give up on the struggle for faith, and the vision of love and the insistence on hope, then the world becomes less palatable to God.

But if the claim and the reality are not to diverge and create a credibility gap of enormous proportions, then two temptations must be avoided. Jewish people long ago used to tell a story about someone who looked back, and they summed the point of the story up in a proverb: 'Remember Lot's wife'. Lot's wife was told that everything would be well if she looked forward. But she looked back, and was turned into a pillar of salt. Sometimes we prefer to be pillars of the church rather than salt for the earth; but pillars of the church can very easily become pillars of salt, forever looking back to old ways and old solutions.

That's one temptation. The other is to believe that the true way to stop the world going bad, and to make the world palatable to God, is to be sweetness and light, to offend nobody, to keep the peace at all costs and put up with everything while standing up for very little. But Jesus told us to be salt for the world. If he had meant sugar, he would have said it.

On a very wet Sunday morning in Rome a few years ago, I was making my way to the only bank open in Rome on a Sunday to cash some travellers' cheques when I passed the ancient ruins of what is called Trajan's Forum. Trajan was a Roman Emperor at the start of the second century, and he had this forum built – it's a public square, a meeting place – to celebrate his victories in war. And towering up from the middle of the square is Trajan's Column – not unlike Nelson's Column in Trafalgar Square. Trajan's Column is 125 feet high, built by the people to honour a great emperor. And on top of the column they put a larger-than-life statue of the Emperor Trajan himself. I suppose it was a cultural version of the tower of Babel!

As I looked to the top of Trajan's Column, I remembered that eighty or so years after the death of Jesus, letters were exchanged between the Emperor Trajan and the governor of one of the far-flung provinces of the Roman Empire. The governor was called Pliny, and Pliny wrote to the Emperor, asking for advice about how to handle a strange new sect he had come across called the Christians. Actually, he knew perfectly well what to do with them. They were to be punished, and, if necessary, executed. But, like a good civil servant, Pliny wanted to cover himself and make sure that he was doing the right thing. So he investigated the Christians, and discovered that all they did when they met in secret was to promise to follow someone called Christ, not to commit crimes, and to eat what Pliny described as 'ordinary and harmless food'. He wanted to know if this bunch of unimportant, eccentric Christians really should be punished so harshly. 'A perverse and extravagant superstition' was how Pliny described Christianity to the Emperor of Rome: Christians were harmless people who posed no threat to anyone.

If you stand in Trajan's Forum today, as I did, and look up at the top of Trajan's Column, you will not see the larger-than-life statue of the Emperor which was originally put there. You will see the statue of a Galilean fisherman called Peter, which replaced the statue of Trajan hundreds of years ago. Poor Pliny got it horribly wrong. And it was a later Emperor than Trajan, but one who had made it his business to try to root out the Christian sect, who died with the words on his lips: 'Thou hast conquered, O Galilean'.

I said that I am reluctant to talk about the Church because of that story T. S. Eliot told about the baker's shop. I am also haunted by something Eliot wrote:

All men are ready to invest their money
but most expect dividends . . .
I say: take no thought of the harvest,
But only of proper sowing.

Seed-sowing is another of the pictures Jesus used to describe what he expected from his followers who became the church on the day of Pentecost. It is frustrating to sow seed on a path among unreceptive people who aren't open to the possibility of anything new or fresh or different – you could say among the doubting Thomases of this world It is disappointing and demoralising to sow seed onto rocks, among the sort of people who are all promises but no action, very ready to follow when things are bright but nowhere to be seen when the going gets tough: rocky people, like the one they called Peter. It is to live with blighted hopes and dreams unfulfilled to sow seed onto thorny ground, where the initial growth is choked, among the sort of people whose ambitions get in the way of their discipleship, and stifle it: like James and John with their upwardly mobile plans.

Maybe the story Jesus told about the sower was his own inner story: the frustration and disappointment he felt at how the seed he had sown *among us his disciples, his followers*, had not done very well. Why did Jesus not just give up? Because Jesus believed passionately in the germinating power of the kingdom. 'Now take a grain of mustard seed. There is no more insignificant seed on earth, but it grows into a shrub with branches so large that the birds of the air can shelter in shade.'

Sowing seed is an image, a picture, in which Jesus meant us to recognise not what so often we think it is about – the seed *we* have to sow and the disappointments *we* have to put up with – but rather the seed he sows among us, to such frustrating effect sometimes. But we need to recognize in the spreading of the seed, which gently lands on the ground, so light that a gust of wind could blow it away, something which is light and gentle, tenuous and delicate and fragile, and learn that the Gospel is not something to bludgeon people with or bully them into believing. The sowing of the Gospel needs a lightness of touch; and, to have any effect, it must touch people's lives gently. As someone who works in religious *broadcasting*, I am constantly aware that the word 'broadcasting' derives from what farmers did with seeds, and that without that lightness of touch we're going to fail to spread the word in a way that will take root. But don't let the seed's fragility fool you into thinking it lacks toughness. Seeds are tough.

For an Easter Sunday, I made a television film with the Glasgow poet Edwin Morgan. On the morning the film was shown, it was announced that Edwin Morgan had been awarded the Queen's Medal for Poetry. I asked Edwin to write some poems for the programme which, in a light way, turned on the theme of resurrection and new life in signs he might have seen in Glasgow.

One of the poems he wrote is called 'Nature':

Abandoned buildings sprout their leaves,
Taking the air on roofs and eaves.
No ledge, no crack is safe from nature,
Opportunism is its feature.
Demolished sites are worse, they're jungles.
No one had bungled, but the bungles
Of grass, cans, trolleys, plastic bags,
Cow-parsley, tyres, fireweed and rags
Are like a field of battle for
The seeds of the green world to floor
Their future forests from. The fight,
Nothing concerned with wrong or right,
Relentless and invisible,
Makes renewal invincible
But leaves a problematic plan
For architecture and for man.

What links the image of the sower sowing the seed with the salt for the world is that both have to be sprinkled. Seeds which are dropped in piles cannot all germinate. Salt applied in thick coatings is horrible. But the Gospel, spread with the same lightness of touch and sensitivity as sprinkling, has a power to transform and renew and restore.

# 9

# All My Hope on God is Founded

WHEN the Hebrew people wanted to find ways of talking about God, they turned to a story about their hero Moses, who was watching his father-in-law's sheep on a hillside when he saw a bush on fire; but the flames of the fire did not burn the bush up (Exodus 3:1–14):

> Then Moses said, 'I must turn aside and look at this great sight, and see why the bush is not burned up.' When the Lord saw that he had turned aside to see, God called to him out of the bush, 'Moses! Moses!' And he said, 'Here I am.' Then he said, 'Come no closer! Remove the sandals from your feet, for the place on which you are standing is holy ground.' He said further, 'I am the God of your father, the God of Abraham, the God of Isaac and the God of Jacob.' And Moses hid his face, for he was afraid to look at God. So God told Moses that he had heard the pain of the Israelites in Egypt, and he wanted Moses to go to Egypt to bring his people to the Promised Land. But Moses said to God, 'If I come to the Israelites and say to them, "The God of your ancestors has sent me to you", and they ask me "What is his name?", what shall I say to them?' God said to Moses, 'I AM WHO I AM.' He said further, 'Thus you shall say to the Israelites, "I AM has sent me to you."'

A representation of the burning bush is the emblem of the Church of Scotland and of many other Presbyterian churches around the world, and it was the French who gave that emblem to Presbyterianism. The Huguenots, the small, brave, frequently persecuted French Protestants, had adopted the burning bush as their emblem, and Scottish ministers who taught in the Huguenot colleges brought the emblem back from France; and it caught on with the Covenanters, who saw themselves as Scottish Huguenots, small in number and frequently persecuted. In 1691, the records of the General Assembly of the Church of Scotland for the first time were printed with a burning bush on the front page, and ever since then the Church of Scotland has used the burning bush as its symbol, with the motto: 'Nec tamen consumebatur', 'And yet, it was not burned up': that bush which Moses caught sight of on the hillside.

There have been all sorts of explanations of why it appeared on fire yet not to be burned up. Perhaps it was a bush in brilliant flower, and the flowers gave the impression of flames? Perhaps at sunset the red rays of the sun fell on a thorn bush and created the effect of fire? Perhaps, but I suspect the writer of the Book of Exodus, who has introduced Moses as someone who has tramped the desert as a shepherd for decades, did not imagine he had been taken in by a bush in bloom or the sun's rays. And I suspect it was not the burning bush which mattered to the writer of Exodus. In the intense heat of the dry desert, a bush catching fire was all too common. Nor was it really even the fact that the bush didn't seem to be burned up that mattered. Appearances can be deceptive, and the curiosity was merely what attracted Moses' attention. Rather, what mattered to the writer of Exodus was the encounter Moses had with God beside the burning bush, in a commonplace sight; but in what was commonplace touched by God, who says to Moses: 'Take off your shoes, for the place where you are standing is holy ground'.

In the days when I was a parish minister, and people used to complain to me about couples who had no connection with the church coming to be married, I used to say that sometimes people need buildings to say for them what they can't say for themselves. Sometimes only places which have been hallowed by time and prayer provide the right setting where people discover in themselves what the poet Philip Larkin calls 'a hunger to be more serious'. But Moses was on holy ground not because it had been consecrated or hallowed but because anywhere can be holy, whenever the commonplace is touched by God.

> Where'er they seek thee, thou art found,
> and every place is hallowed ground.

An old priest on the Hebridean island of South Uist told an interviewer in a Gaelic television programme that as a schoolboy, in the springtime of every year, he used to take off his boots and go everywhere barefoot. 'I thought I could feel the ground coming alive under my feet after the long winter sleep. And then in the autumn I could feel it getting ready to die again.' And then the old man turned away to look out of his kitchen window over the machair to the Atlantic breakers, and then he muttered: 'I say all these sorts of things in Gaelic because in English they just sound daft'.

They wouldn't have sounded daft to the poet Elizabeth Barrett Browning, who wrote:

> Earth's crammed with heaven
> and every common bush afire with God.
> But only he who sees takes off his shoes
> The rest sit round it and pick blackberries.

Take off your shoes: first of all because it is a mark of respect and a sign of humility. We must be respectful towards and humble before God, of course, but also respectful and humble in the presence of that place where suddenly it all became clear, or that moment when everything was crystallised or that time which was beyond time. Let there be respect and humility for that moment which has transported us beyond time and place. We all of us have moments, experiences, flashes of insight, glimpses of truth which we cannot really describe; but for me they are the moments when for a brief time everything is clear. And then of course the moment passes, just as on the Mount of Transfiguration the moment passed for the disciples Jesus had taken with him up the hill. Do not be tempted to dismiss these moments as 'mere emotion' – as if those moments when we experience reality, truth or God *emotionally* are less convincing than the moments when we understand things logically. For millions of years since we emerged on this planet, we have experienced things emotionally. We have only understood things logically since the Greeks discovered logic 3,000 years ago. Take off your shoes. Because it's a mark of respect and a sign of humility.

Secondly, taking off your shoes is a symbol of status and a sign of poverty. I cherish the remark someone made about the former Prime Minister, Harold Wilson. He had been going on at some length about the bad old days when his family were so poor that he had to go to school in his bare feet. And someone said: 'If Harold Wilson went to school in his bare feet, it was just because he was too big for his boots'! Going barefoot is an indication of the poverty that can't afford shoes.

Now let us be clear. When Jesus said 'Blessed are the poor', he was not saying that there is anything good about poverty. When he said that it is easier for a camel to go through the eye of a needle than for a rich person to enter the Kingdom of God, he was not damning to all eternity everyone who is rich, otherwise you and I, whatever our circumstances, in comparison to the peasant in Bangladesh or the ground worker in Guatemala or the refugee in Macedonia, are rich and must be lost. When he said 'Blessed are the poor', Jesus was making a point about the attitude which poverty induces and the approach which wealth encourages. The poor are not tempted to rely on the things of this world, because they do not have any of the things of the world. They are much more likely to be open to a kingdom which is not of this world, because they are much less likely to put their trust in the things of this world. Poor people are much more likely to realise that the Kingdom of God is as close as the first step they take towards it because they are not likely to grasp what they know they don't have.

And take off your shoes, because, thirdly, it is evidence of relaxation and a sign of being at ease. After you have climbed a hill, or hiked across a moor, or trudged up a mountain path, and you come across one of these lochans that do not appear on any map, and you decide to stop, and even before you dip your feet in the ice-cold water, you've let the air blow around your feet: there is no experience quite like it for easing the exhaustion and making you relaxed.

How many versions of faith, how many forms of religion, how many expressions of Christianity stress discipline, obedience and restraint, and expect our lives to be brought under control and in check?

Alan Spence is one of Scotland's finest contemporary writers. He has written a book of short stories all about the Glasgow I grew up in during the 1950s, and it is wonderfully evocative of those days. There is one story about a wee boy called Aleck, being 'got ready' (as they used to say) for Sunday school. But in the way it is told, it is actually about the kind of harsh, uptight, disciplined form of religion that was taught there. 'His mother laid out his shirt and his suit, his heavy shoes and a pair of clean white ankle socks. This was the horrible part, the part that was really disgusting. The clothes made him feel so stiff and uncomfortable. Slowly, sadly, he put them on. The shoes were solid polished black leather, and he consciously clumped around the kitchen. He found it impossible to feel at ease.' And the story ends with Aleck running home from Sunday school: 'Suddenly he laughed and started off towards home. His dinner would be ready. He would change into his old clothes and after he had eaten he would go and play till it was dark.'[20]

In December 1998, I went to Harare in Zimbabwe for a meeting of the World Council of Churches. One of the keynote speeches was delivered by a theological hero of mine, a Japanese theologian called Kosuke Koyama. And he turned everything I've been saying on its head. Because, he said, it is God who is barefoot. 'The whole world', he said, 'is now holy ground. We remove our sandals. Grace is barefoot.' It is amazing grace. For grace is the sign of a God who is humble, the God who the prophet Isaiah said would not break a crushed reed (or, as we would say today, 'wouldn't hurt a fly'), the God who the Letter to the Philippians says 'humbled himself and made himself nothing'.

And grace is the sign of a God who is poor, the God who, according to the Psalms, 'always stands at the right hand of the poor', and who, as St Paul wrote to his friends at Corinth, 'became poor for our sakes'. And grace is the sign of the God who is at ease with us, who, when we approach him anxious and uptight because we're not good enough, says: 'Let's have a feast and kill the fatted calf' and who, when we've exhausted ourselves trying to prove how valuable we are, says: 'Just come and join the party'. God is barefoot: the humble God who exalts the meek and the lowly, the God of the poor who nevertheless makes many rich, the God who is at ease with us, yet who asks of us justice and righteousness.

A Roman Catholic priest once told me that he had been talking to a primary school class, asking the pupils the questions in the Catholic catechism. Every question the priest asked was answered by a horribly bright young boy in the front row. After a while, the priest came to the question 'Where is God?', and the boy answered: 'God is everywhere'. The correct answer again. But by this time the priest had got a bit annoyed with his questions being answered not only so accurately but so smugly that he decided it was time the boy got his come-uppance. 'That's right', he said. 'God *is* everywhere. But where is everywhere?' There was a moment's silence, and then the boy answered: 'I don't know, but my mother says that you can get a bus for everywhere on Princes Street'.

You and I think that if we want to know something about another person we need to get to know all about them. 'Getting to know you', as the old song puts it. 'Getting to know all about you.' But in the world of the Bible, where a person *was to be found* told you much more about them than any amount of descriptions of what sort of person they were. A couple of years ago, someone who I thought I knew quite well took me to the place in the Western Isles of Scotland where his family came from. I realised then that you might be able to take him out of the Western Isles, and transplant him into Edinburgh, but you could not ever take the Western Isles out of him. Observing him on the island revealed more than I had ever known about him. Perhaps the notion, the idea, the belief that what is important about someone isn't who they are, but where they are most at home, is not as strange as it seems. And so, when the Bible wants to say something revealing about God, it doesn't try to describe or define who God is. If we go back to the story of Moses and the burning bush, in which God tells Moses to go down to Egypt and free the Israelites, Moses asks God: 'And who exactly am I to say has sent me?' And the voice of God says to Moses: 'Just say "I am". Just say: "I am" has sent you.' Scholars have argued about that puzzling answer for a long time. It is the name that the Jewish people gave to God. 'I am.' Not so long ago, a friend of mine shed quite a lot of light on the name, for he says that if you want to understand what it means you should think of God saying (more familiarly if less grammatically): 'It's me'. Think of a child who wakens up in the middle of the night with a bad dream, or frightened by a thunderstorm, confused and frightened and crying. What does a parent do? She holds the child close and says: 'It's all right. It's me.' When I was making a radio programme shortly after the death of Cardinal Gordon Gray, the Roman Catholic Archbishop of St Andrews and Edinburgh, I was told that when he phoned people who knew him well he invariably introduced himself by saying simply: 'It's myself'.

And maybe all that any of us can say about God is that at the centre of the universe and at the heart of life, in the midst of our questionings and in the middle of our experience, there is God, simply saying and saying simply: 'It's me'.

What is God like? Who is God? How can you describe the indescribable or define the indefinable? You will not actually find many answers to these questions in the Bible because, irritatingly, when you ask questions to which the Bible does not have the answer, you are simply told that you are asking the wrong question. And so, instead of replying to 'What is God like?', the Bible prefers to answer a different question: 'Where is God to be found, where is God at home?' In telling us something about that, it gives us glimpses of what God is like. People of Christian faith, who believe (as St Paul puts it) that 'God was in Christ', will find very few answers to questions about who Jesus was, or what Jesus was like, or how to define his relationship to God. But we will find answers aplenty to the question of where Jesus was to be found, where Jesus was at home. Nearly sixty years ago, the German teacher and martyr Dietrich Bonhoeffer said that the one question we should be asking is: 'Who is Christ for us today?' But maybe we cannot answer that question until we ask: 'Where is Christ for us today?'

So, where do the Gospels say Jesus was to be found? He once said to his disciples: 'Where two or three are gathered together in my name, there am I in the midst of them'. Down the ages, countless Christians who have gathered for worship or for prayer have found that to be true. Even where there are just a few, there is Christ with them. When St Matthew wrote about two or three being gathered together in Christ's name, he was not thinking of them gathering for worship or for prayer or for devotions. He was actually thinking of two or three Christians (or many more, but two or three was a quorum) meeting together to take decisions on behalf of the Christian community. What Jesus said, according to Matthew, was a deliberate echo of part of the Jewish law, which said: 'Where two or three are sitting together, *and studying the words of the law*, the glory of God rests on them'. When people reach decisions which are Christian, in Christ's name, in a Christlike way, there is Christ in the midst of them.

Some years ago, Professor Donald MacLeod of the Free Church of Scotland was the subject of a series of attacks on his integrity and character from inside his own Church. After he was finally acquitted of all the charges against him, he was asked what lessons he had learned, and he said that his experience had taught him that very often 'those who were least orthodox were sometimes most Christian, and those who were least Christian were often most orthodox'. That is exactly why Jesus made that important change to what was said about the law. It was not people discussing how orthodox they were on whom the glory of God was shed, but those who were Christlike in their approach and their attitude and their dealings who found Christ present with them. Where is Christ for us today? Where two or three are gathered together in his name.

One night when the disciples were out in a boat, and a storm blew up, and their fragile craft was being beaten by waves, 'In the fourth watch of the night he came to them saying, "Take heart. It is I."' The late Professor Willie Barclay, whose daughter was drowned while sailing on a Northern Ireland loch, said in a broadcast about that incident, that when the Gospels report that Jesus stilled the storm, 'If Jesus stilled a storm once upon a time, that doesn't mean very much to me. But if every time people are battered by the storm of life – the cold, bleak wind of sorrow or the hot blast of passion or the storm of doubt – and then they find Jesus to be alongside them, that is much more important.'

However, one word of warning. Often when we are going through the mill, or when the storms are round us, we sense no helping presence, no sustaining power. Often it is only after-wards that we realise we have been sustained by the One who is closest when the need is greatest but perhaps sensed then the least. This is why the teacher Kierkegaard said that although life had to be lived forwards it could only be understood backwards. Where is Christ for us today? 'In every pang that rends the heart, the Man of Sorrows has a part.'

For Jesus' disciples, what Willie Barclay described as the bleak winds of sorrow and the storms of doubt blew most keenly and most sharply that Friday outside Jerusalem, and in the dark hours which followed. When the women went to the hollow rock and found it empty, they were told: 'Go and tell his disciples and Peter that he is going ahead of you into Galilee and will meet you there'. Whenever, despite hurt and loss and pain and disappointment, we go back to Galilee where faith once was fresh and young and vibrant and full of excitement, Christ is there for us today. Whenever, despite any guilt we live with or shame we know, we go back to Galilee and try to rediscover the brightness of a new loyalty and the tender innocence of a new love, there Christ is for us today. Whenever, despite the worst that the world can do and the bitterness that experience can bring, we go back to Galilee and risk hoping again and trusting again and believing again, Christ is there for us today, saying perhaps: 'It's me', as to the leper and the outcast, as to the widow and the prostitute, as to the disciples who failed him and went fishing to escape. That voice said: 'It's me', and is with us to the end of time.

Because of what the Hebrew people had learned about the God who described himself as I AM, and because of what Christian people had learned about the God they encountered through Christ, both made enemies. The Hebrew people made enemies of the Babylonians, who expanded their empire throughout the Middle East because they wanted power. Later on, the people of Israel made enemies of the Greeks, whose empire planted Greek civilisation everywhere because it reflected what the Greeks believed about truth. And later still, the people of Israel made enemies of the Romans when they would not fit neatly into an empire which was based on law and order. But the strange thing about the people of Israel is that they didn't make enemies of those who wanted power because they wanted power for themselves. They did not make enemies of those who pursued truth because truth didn't matter to them. They did not make enemies of those who promised law and order because they preferred some kind of anarchy. The people of Israel made enemies because, instead of being obsessed by power, or truth, or law and order, they were gripped by a different obsession. Very simply, they were obsessed by this God who had met Moses beside the burning bush.

I once heard the General Assembly of the Church of Scotland being told the story of a dancer on the New York stage who was rehearsing her dance when she was told by the theatre management that she was sacked. But she just danced on. 'Don't you hear me?' the theatre manager shouted. 'You're fired!' But she just danced on. Again he shouted: 'You're fired!' He yelled even louder, but she still danced on, saying very quietly to the theatre manager: 'You can't fire an artist, because we dance for a different employer.' The Church of Jesus Christ has always danced for a different employer; and so, down through the ages, the Church has made enemies. It has made enemies of exactly the same sort of people as the people of Israel did. The early Church made enemies of those who wanted power and was persecuted by those who saw Christianity as a threat. It made enemies of those who pursued truth and who could not disguise their contempt for this pathetic religion which chose to follow a crucified carpenter. It made enemies of those who promoted law and order because Christianity was thought to be disturbing the peace.

And what was the response of the early Christians to all of this? In the face of persecution, they laughed at the pretensions of power; and whenever they were mocked for this crude belief that God could be present in someone who was crucified, they just continued to meet together in the belief that God was still present in the symbols of the crucified One's body and blood; and whenever they were accused of being disruptive and

condemned to death, they simply knelt and asked that God
would forgive their enemies. They were not taken in by power,
or convinced by reason, or afraid of death. They were simply
obsessed with God. The doctrine of the Trinity is the result of
the obsession the early Christians had with God. As John Henry
Newman wrote,

> Firmly I believe and truly
> God is Three and God is One.

In the days before mathematics and I parted company – and
I have to admit that we never really got very well acquainted – I
had to learn geometry. I had to learn and be able to write down
on an examination paper things like the proof of Pythagoras'
theorem about the square on the hypotenuse of a right-angled
triangle. And while I think I might just be able to recognise a
right-angled triangle, I'm not sure I would know a hypotenuse
if I encountered one! But I passed the geometry examination by
realising that I did not have to understand all of it so long as I
could memorise the formulas and write them down. If anyone
asked me what they meant, I was lost! It is tempting to think
that God has been boiled down to a formula – Three in One and
One in Three – as incomprehensible as geometry was to me.
We'll sing about it, but we'll be lost if we're asked what it
means. But originally, the idea of the Trinity was worked out to
describe and to safeguard the early Christians' obsession with
God. And then the theologians took over.

It was a theologian's sermon which has helped me to
understand the experience which the Trinity was meant to
express. Professor John McIntyre once said, very simply, that
to believe in the Trinity means to believe in God, here, there and
everywhere.

God here. The German poet Heinrich Heine once stood with a friend in front of the cathedral at Amiens in France. 'Tell me, Heinrich,' said his friend, 'why can't we build cathedrals like this any more?' And Heinrich answered: 'Because in those days people had convictions, and today all we have are opinions, and it takes more than opinions to build a cathedral.' What set fire to the imagination of the early Christians was much more than opinions about God, but the conviction that God was intensely real to them in the heat of their own experience, the burning conviction that God mattered.

Whenever Harold Wilson wanted to tell the British Labour Party that it was having one of its internal discussions which were irrelevant to the lives of ordinary people, he would say that it was 'just talking theology'. The great wartime Archbishop of Canterbury, William Temple, once said: 'Whenever I talk about theology, they say I am irrelevant; and whenever I talk about social issues, they say I am interfering'. But the faith which convinced the early Christians to be obsessed about God was a faith in a God who was so relevant that what they believed about him kept interfering with everything they thought and said and did. God here. As near to them as breathing, and just as vital.

And God there: in the life and death and resurrection of Jesus of Nazareth. Of course Jesus talked about God; but what made the hairs on the backs of the necks of these early Christians stand up and tingle with excitement was the conviction that Jesus had not just been talking about God but had been God among them. In the ordinariness of living, this was God. In the extraordinariness of living a life of love, this was God. In the downright amazement of living a life of love which accepted no limits and knew no bounds, this was God. God here in their experience. God there in their experience.

And God everywhere in their experience. That is exactly what the writer of the Psalm understood about the spirit of God. 'Where can I go from your spirit? Or where can I flee from your presence? If I ascend to heaven, you are there; if I make my bed in Sheol you are there. If I take the wings of the morning and settle at the farthest limits of the sea, even there your hand shall lead me, and your right hand shall hold me fast.' Or, as one of the great figures of the early Church, St Augustine, put it: God is a circle whose centre is everywhere and whose circumference is nowhere.

God here, there and everywhere. That is what the early Christians believed, and therefore they made enemies. They made enemies of those who wanted power – because, if God was here and now, then there was no other power who had an ultimate claim on their lives. 'I am the Lord, there is no other', says God. They made enemies of those who pursued truth because those who pursued truth thought that it was a fine intellectual game which they could take their time playing. But Christians said that the truth they had discovered was a matter of life and death which people had better attend to urgently. 'I am the way, the truth and the life', said Jesus. And they made enemies of those who promoted law and order and who liked the world to be well organised and controlled, because their God was as free as the wind, and the wind blows where it will and cannot be controlled. 'I will pour out my spirit on all', said the first Pentecost sermon.

They made enemies, these early Christians, because they were obsessed with God: the God they had sensed here in the Father who never abandoned them, there in the Son who revealed God to them, everywhere in the Spirit who made them free.

No doubt there are some Christians who will want to go

much further than I have done in describing the doctrine of
the Trinity as an expression of the experience of the early
Christians. They will want to say that the doctrine of the Trinity
describes the very nature of God himself. 'God in three Persons,
blessed Trinity', as the hymn puts it. I cannot myself go along
with those who take that view, and in support of my reticence I
want to quote two people who are from diametrically opposed
points on the spectrum of belief. The first is Professor James
S. Stewart, a much-loved Scottish teacher and preacher whose
heyday was in the 1940s and 1950s. He once said that the
doctrine of the Trinity came into being when the early
Christians discovered that they could not say all that they meant
by 'God' until they said 'Father, Son and Holy Spirit', and he
went on to describe what the early Christians meant by 'Father,
Son and Holy Spirit' in terms of their experience of the Father's
forgiveness, the Son's love and the fellowship of the Holy
Spirit.

When I talked to Bishop Jack Spong for a radio programme,
he said this:

> I don't think that God is a Trinity because I can't tell you
> what God is like. I can tell you that I have experienced God
> as 'infinite Other', and that's what 'Father' means. I have
> experienced God as the depth within, and that's what 'Spirit'
> means. And I have experienced God incarnate in human life
> and most particularly in the life of the one I call 'my Lord',
> and so I experience God in these three ways, and I say to
> myself that the only way I can make sense of that is to say
> that I am a Trinitarian, but I don't think that is what God is
> like, and I'm not going to tell anyone that I've captured God
> in the formulas of my faith. I think the Church must play
> loose with its dogmas and its doctrines.

The doctrine of the Trinity is described, classically, in the Creed which is named after the early theologian Athanasius: 'The Catholic faith is this: that we worship one God in Trinity, and Trinity in Unity; neither confounding the Persons nor dividing the Substance. For there is one Person of the Father, another of the Son and another of the Holy Ghost. But the Godhead of the Father, and of the Son and of the Holy Ghost, is all one: the Glory equal, the Majesty co-eternal.'

One of the men from whom I learned to love the study of the New Testament, Professor Dennis Nineham, used to like quoting a phrase of the scholar Leonard Hodgson: 'What must the truth be now if people who thought as the biblical writers did, put it like that'.

# 10

# Band of Hope

MY father was minister of Stevenson Memorial Church in Glasgow, and on its sixtieth anniversary there was a communion service at which Lord Reith, the founder of the BBC, whose father had been the first minister of the church, read from the Bible, and the then Moderator of the General Assembly, Dr Archie Craig, preached. I remember the service vividly because, characteristically, Lord Reith announced that he was dissatisfied with all the translations of the passages he was asked to read and that he had made his own translation; but also because of the sermon Archie Craig preached. I can recall the text, a story and a quotation from that sermon. The text was from the book of Revelation, chapter 22 verse 31: 'The grace of our Lord Jesus Christ be with you all'. What is the grace of Jesus Christ? Think of what the Gospels tell us about Jesus. They say he had power: all sorts of power. Power to heal people, power over the winds and the waves, power to forgive sins. The Gospels say Jesus had compassion. When the crowds had nothing to eat, Jesus had compassion on them. When the son of a widow died, he had compassion for her. When a blind man asked for sight, he had compassion on him. And love. The clever young lawyer who asked Jesus a trick question – 'looking at him, Jesus loved him'. The one family he was closest to in Bethany – 'Jesus loved Martha, and her sister, and Lazarus'. And, of course, his disciples – 'having loved his own, he loved them to the end'.

Power. Compassion. Love. And you could go on adding to the list. But 'grace' isn't just something else to be added to all the gifts and the qualities and the characteristics of Jesus. Grace isn't another attribute or virtue. Grace is the way all the qualities Jesus displayed are expressed, conveyed and communicated. So the power of Jesus is expressed in a way that does not threaten people or exploit them or reduce them to being dependent. A friend of mine, who suffers from time to time from crippling depression, finds it very difficult then to accept help. 'The last thing I need', he once told me, 'when I'm weak is to be threatened by people who seem to have got it all together'. But the power of Jesus was enabling, not enslaving. And the compassion of Jesus is conveyed in a way that does not patronise people or demean them or make them dependent. I was once talking to the late Professor Willie Barclay about someone who he knew disliked him intensely. And he said to me: 'I can't think why. Because I don't think I've ever helped him.' But the compassion of Jesus brought restoration and not resentment. And the love of Jesus is communicated in a way that is unconditional, hoping for love to be returned but demanding nothing, and enduring the hurt that love endures but loving still. It was once said of an apparently saintly Christian: 'Yes, he loves people all right. You can tell that by their hunted look.' But the love of Jesus was offered, not oppressive. The grace of the Lord Jesus Christ. It is the manner in which the power and compassion and love of Jesus were expressed and conveyed and communicated.

Archie Craig lived until he was well into his nineties. And during his last years, he looked after his wife, who suffered from senile dementia. A friend of mine, who only met Archie Craig towards the end of his life, once asked him how he coped with a wife who barely knew him. And Archie Craig replied: 'I'm having to learn a whole new alphabet of love'. I wish I could always hear from Christians today something which reflected the grace of the Lord Jesus Christ, something of that new alphabet of love which God employs to communicate with us. Which brings me to the story which Archie Craig told in that sermon. It was a story about a celebrated preacher of a past generation called Murray McCheyne. One Monday, McCheyne asked a brother minister what his text had been the day before, and was told with grimly set lips that it had been Psalm 9 verse 17: 'The wicked shall be turned into hell'. And McCheyne asked gently: 'And were you able to preach *affectionately* from that text?' I wish, when I hear some Christians talking about the power of Jesus Christ, I could hear much more of the power which enabled people to be the people it was in them to be, and less of the power to condemn them for who they are. In other words, I wish I heard more of the grace of the Lord Jesus Christ. I wish, when I hear some people expressing the compassion they had learned from Jesus Christ, I could hear more of Christ's compassion for everyone – outcasts and sinners and reprobates – and less about how, because of the compassion they feel for some, they feel the need to attack and judge others. In other words, I wish I heard more of the grace of the Lord Jesus Christ. I wish, when I hear Christians preaching about the love of God, I could hear that God so loved the world, the world which rejected him and denied him and crucified him, and less about a God who extends his welcome only to those who believe, only to those who have signed up in his cause. In other words, I wish I heard more of the grace of the Lord Jesus Christ.

I hear people saying that the Church is declining because preachers are not aggressively preaching the Gospel, or because schools will not allow Christians to evangelise, or because ministers have become like social workers, caring for people without sticking a religious label on their care, or because the Church has become committed to meeting the world's needs without demanding the world's faith in return. When people say these sorts of things to me, I wish they would realise that what is required of Christians is that they live out the grace of Jesus Christ – his considerateness for others, his patience, his availability to everyone, his tact, his manner of forgiveness, his courage. It is by who we are that we communicate the grace of the Lord Jesus Christ. But we will only communicate the grace of the Lord Jesus Christ if we have known it ourselves; if we have stopped trying to win God's approval and simply accepted his love; if we have stopped trying to justify ourselves to God and simply accepted the fact that God has accepted us; if we have stopped imagining God as a stern parent and realised that he is a vulnerable, loving Father. And sometimes that is all very difficult for us to understand because it goes against everything we usually believe. 'You get nothing for nothing.' 'You have to earn respect.' 'You have to deserve rewards.' 'You must work for anything you get.' And the grace of God is about turning all of that on its head. Everything for nothing. Respect we've done nothing to earn. Rewards we aren't entitled to. But we can insulate ourselves against all of this. Like the person learning to swim, who sinks to the bottom because he tenses and stiffens up, and will not trust the buoyancy of the water, we can resist the grace of God ourselves and turn religion into something which is all about what we must do, become so preoccupied with it, so tense and uptight about it. Then we will never convey that grace which is like the buoyant water sustaining those who trust it.

This is maybe what the hymn-writer John Newton had in mind – he was after all a ship's captain and presumably knew a

thing or two about swimming – when he linked the grace of
God to the living waters which spring from eternal love:

Grace, which like the Lord the giver
Never fails from age to age.

One other thing Archie Craig said in that sermon sticks in my
mind. He reminded us that when we speak about a person being
'gracious' we mean a combination of courtesy and kindness and
sympathy which make up a warm personality. And then he said
that he had once heard it said in a sermon that it would do
Christians the world of good if, now and again in reading the
New Testament, they were to substitute the word 'charm' for
the word 'grace'. 'May the charm of the Lord Jesus Christ be
visible to you all.'

When I was a small boy, I developed quite an admiration for
the Jesus who appears in the story that Luke tells about what
happened to Jesus when he was 12 years old. But the admiration had nothing to do with anything that Luke wanted us to
learn from the story; it had more to do with the fact that Jesus
appeared to have escaped from his family and got away with it.

I had tried the same thing. It was a school half-holiday, I
think, and a friend of mine who lived in Dennistoun asked me
if I wanted to go back to his house and play. And of course I said
'Yes'; and when we got to his house, his mother quite naturally
asked if my parents knew where I was. And of course I said
'Yes'. We lived at the time in the west end of Glasgow, which
then was about as far from Dennistoun as you could get, and
for several hours that afternoon my parents contacted all the
friends I had close to our home, and they searched the streets,
and eventually they contacted the police, and it was only much

later towards evening, when I appeared remarkably reluctant to go home, that the penny dropped with my friend's mother, and she phoned my parents and the truth came out. Our family did not own a car; so, when he came home from work, my friend's father discovered that he had to drive me across the city, rather more quickly than I remember wanting him to, and so back home, where my mother expressed tearful relief at the return of her first-born, and my father expressed a more hostile and, to me, much more painful reaction. So I developed this admiration for the Jesus in Luke's story who appeared to have avoided the consequences of his disappearance in a way that, painfully, I did not.

That is one of the stories that always get retold about me at family gatherings. You know the sort of thing. When the only thing that people have got in common any more is the past, the easiest kind of conversation is the kind that begins: 'Do you remember the time when . . . ?' And I've always thought that the stories which are remembered actually tell you more about the person who has apparently remembered them and treasured them than they tell you about the person who figures in the story.

This story about Jesus going to the Temple at the age of 12, and getting lost, was apparently remembered and treasured by the early Christians. Apart from the stories surrounding his birth, it is the only thing any of the Gospels tell us about Jesus from the time he was born until the time he set out on his ministry. So why was it remembered? What does the fact that this is the only story that has been preserved about Jesus' boyhood and adolescence tell us about the faith of these early Christians?

There were all sorts of stories going the rounds about the boyhood of Jesus: stories like the one about him making model birds out of the muddy clay beside a road one Sabbath. A

Pharisee came past and told Jesus to stop what he was doing because making models on the Sabbath was breaking the commandment. And Jesus said: 'I will not', and he clapped his hands and the clay birds came to life and flew away. Lots of stories like that one were going the rounds when Luke wrote his Gospel; but Luke does not recount any of them, because they are fanciful and fantastic and obviously apocryphal and they convey the picture of a child wonder-worker. Instead, Luke tells this story of two parents who lose their child. In contrast to all these other legends, this story is so typical: not just in the sense that children do get lost and their parents do get anxious, but typical in the sense that parents do have to lose their children in adolescence. Perhaps this story could say that they have to lose their children in adolescence in order to find them again. And that's something that any parent will recognise.

One of my favourite poems was written by C. Day Lewis. It is about going to watch his son playing football; and, after the match, as he sees his son walking away from him, that becomes a powerful symbol of a bigger growing away.

> I have had worse partings, but none that so
> Gnaws at my mind still. Perhaps it is roughly
> Saying what God alone could perfectly show
> How selfhood begins with a walking away
> And love is proved in the letting go.

Maybe this story survived because it said something very real to the early Christians about how their Christian life was about walking away: walking away from fanciful images of Jesus as the miracle-worker, the wonder-worker, the larger-than-life Son of God who would always be there for them, always on hand like the parent of a child to bandage the cuts and soothe the bruises and patch up the wounded egos. Like Jesus, they had to walk away. Like Jesus, their faith has to grow up and find itself. So he stayed in the Temple, asking questions.

He had been taken to the Temple that time, when he was 12, because it was time for his Bar Mitzvah. It was (and still is) a tremendously important moment for Jewish parents. Bar Mitzvah means 'Son of the Law', and at the age of 12 a Jewish boy took on responsibility. He was not a minor any more. His parents were not responsible any more for making sure that he kept the law. His parents could relax. They had done all that they could for their child. It was up to him now.

And there were plenty of people around the early Church who still in a way thought like that. They had not quite managed yet to walk away from the old faith, the old religion. They were still tied to the old notion that if you kept the Jewish law then that was the best that could be expected of you. And I think this story was preserved because it said something very powerful to these early Christians about how that was not enough. There had to be a walking away if they were going to become mature adults in the faith. And like Jesus, when they walked away they began to discover that a mature faith was about a lot more than obedience to the law. It was about discovering what it means to call God 'Father'. So Jesus says to his parents, when eventually they find him: 'Did you not know that I was bound to be in my father's house?'

The playwright John Mortimer some time ago wrote a play called *A Voyage round my Father*. In the play, he explores how as he grew and changed and developed, his understanding of his father grew and changed and developed. Growing up is an exercise in discovering who your parents really are, discovering the people beneath the parental surface and the surface veneer. Maturing in faith has to do with exploring what it means to discover God as your father, and learning from the experience of Jesus what it means to call God 'Father'.

So what *does* it mean? If you read Luke's Gospel, you will find that the word 'Father' comes into the story of the last days of Jesus' life more than it does in any other of the Gospels. 'Father, if you are willing, let this cup pass from me.' 'Father, forgive them, for they don't know what they are doing.' 'Father, into your hands I commit my spirit.' What has all of that, which comes at the very end of the Gospel, got to do with this story about Jesus getting lost, which comes at the very beginning of the Gospel? It has everything to do with it, for there are strange connections between this story at the beginning of the Gospel and the way the Gospel ends. Both happened at Passover time. Luke says that, when Jesus went to the Temple at the age of 12, it was at the time of Passover; and, of course, the crucifixion comes at Passover time. Both involve the Temple, where at the age of 12 Jesus questions the doctors of the law and in the last week of his life he throws out the money-changers. Both involve getting lost for three days: 'After three days they found him sitting in the temple' ... 'Remember how he told you', says the angel to the women at the empty tomb, 'remember how he told you that he must be crucified and must rise again on the third day.' Both involve a question that should not have needed to be asked: 'Why did you search for me? Did you not know I was bound to be in my Father's house?', Jesus says to his parents. 'Why are you searching for the living among the dead?', the angel asks the women at the tomb.

What is the connection? Why is there a story at the start of the Gospel which foreshadows its end, and events at the end of the Gospel which echo this story at the beginning? Because discovering what it means to call God 'Father' is to discover that God's way is always the way of death and resurrection, old life and new life. That is the way God works in our lives. And so the mature faith does not look to the God who prevents suffering and anxiety and problems, but to the God who, whatever happens, is always bringing hope out of despair, and faith out of confusion and life out of death. For that is the nature of this Father's love.

And so, maybe this story of Jesus at the age of 12, with all these hints and echoes of what was to come, was preserved and treasured as if to say to those reading the Gospel right through: read it always with this in mind, that all of this story is the story of death and resurrection, death and resurrection, death and resurrection. And that's the story of your lives too, for that is what we have discovered God is like.

Some years ago, my friend Andrew McLellan nearly drowned when on holiday in California. He would have drowned if a remarkable 16-year-old lifeguard hadn't run quarter of a mile when she heard cries for help, and then plunged into the waves and swum another quarter of a mile and dragged him back to shore. And then she disappeared. He was not able to thank her, and he never met her again until a few years ago, when this lifeguard turned up in Edinburgh. So we filmed their meeting. And then a colleague of mine took Andrew back to the beach in California where it had all happened. They filmed an interview with him there. And the first question to him was this: 'Is it frightening being back where you nearly lost your life?' 'No: because although this is where I nearly lost my life, it's where I had my life given back to me again.' (By a strange irony, Andrew would have conducted the marriage of his lifeguard had he not been due to fly to California for the ceremony on September 12th, the day after the attack on the Twin Towers, when no flights were allowed to operate within United States air space.)

Luke tells this story with its hints of what is to come because he believes that the Gospel is all about saying to people who've been prepared to take the risk of losing their lives that even as they do that, God is giving them their lives back again, renewed and restored.

In St Giles' Cathedral in Edinburgh, the great west window, which in many cathedrals celebrates the saints or apostles, commemorates the poet Robert Burns, whose appearances in church were more often to answer charges of sexual immorality than to display deep piety, and whose poems often satirised the Church of his day and contemporary religious beliefs. And now he is remembered in the west window of the cathedral church of Scottish Presbyterianism.

The minister of St Giles' Cathedral, Gilleasbuig Macmillan, tells how, after he had preached about the story of the prodigal son in a school, a parent told him that he ought to have said to the young people that the prodigal son's father gave him a good hiding. And when the minister pointed out that this was the very opposite of the point of the story, the woman, undaunted, said that people should not get the impression that they could do all sorts of bad things and not be punished for them.

> Later in the conversation, she tackled me on the decision to install a window in St Giles' Cathedral in memory of Robert Burns. A great poet he may have been, and the maker of love-ly songs, but how on earth could I justify a tribute in a Christian church to a man whose relationships with women were so notoriously unchaste? As I prepared to murmur some placatory defence (it was late on a Sunday evening and I didn't feel like an argument), her husband said quietly: 'The prodigal son?' 'Exactly', said I, with relief.

Once, in church, Robert Burns saw a louse crawling up the hat of a lady who was sitting in the pew in front of him. He wrote a poem about it which contains two of Burns' most famous lines:

O wad some Pow'r the giftie gie us
To see oursels as others see us!

But that is only half the problem. What others see in us is just as flawed, just as distorted and just as false as whatever our eyes tell us about other people. Our eyes may see the brash, self-confident image which somebody projects, but not the awful insecurity which lies behind the image and perhaps causes it. Our eyes may envy the bright, sparkling, effervescent personality, but not the loneliness and the pain and the self-doubt which the sparkle disguises. We may wish that we could possess the 'on-top-of-it-all' approach which somebody further up the ladder seems to have, but fail to realise the mass of tensions and contradictions which it hides. We all see the same as everyone else, but God sees why – which explains why God's judgement of people is very different from ours.

So, how can we see ourselves more clearly – not, as Robert Burns wanted, 'as others see us', but as God sees us? Jesus believed that it was by listening to stories: not the sort of stories we tell ourselves about ourselves, in which we reinterpret the past in the best of all possible lights, so that we can comfortably live with our past, but stories about ordinary people in ordinary situations, which don't flatter us or threaten us but in which Jesus asks us to recognise ourselves: like the story of the prodigal son.

I wonder if you have ever asked yourself a question about that story? Why was it that one of the sons turned out to be a thriftless wastrel, while his elder brother turned out to be cold, unwelcoming and jealous? Did each of them suspect that his father didn't love him? That sometimes happens; and, when people feel they are being starved of affection, they very often do one of two things. Sometimes they keep asking for what they think are signs of love. 'Give me what I want and I'll know that you love me.' 'Just do what I ask and I'll be sure that you love me.' We don't actually say it as openly as that, but very often that is what is going on in our heads. We're wanting proof that we are loved. And so the younger son says to his father: 'Give me what you've promised to me, and give it to me now'. Did he want his inheritance as tangible proof of his father's love? And when he gets his share of the inheritance, and goes off to the far country, what does he do? He does what a lot of people do, who have been starved of affection: he tries to buy other people's love, splashing his money around in the hope that it would make people love him, or paying for sex as a substitute for affection. And, of course, it doesn't work. Affection, friendship and respect can't be bought.

There is something else people do when they think they aren't loved: they work themselves to the bone to make sure that they are needed. They slave away, hoping to become indispensable so that they will be wanted and cherished and valued, if not for themselves then for what they do. Is that what the elder brother was all about? Out in the fields till all hours of night, toiling round the clock to keep the farm going, never taking a rest or a holiday. 'The farm won't run itself, you know.' 'Can't afford to take a moment off.' Had the elder brother got it into his head that his father really didn't value him very much for himself, so he would work to be valued for the hours he put in? That doesn't work either. No amount of effort can make someone love you, and there is a world of difference between being valued and being loved.

So perhaps the two brothers in Jesus' story represent two

types of people: those whose insecurity makes them want constant proof that they are loved, and those who try to earn the love they long for. People who need constant reassurance that they are loved are often very insecure about God. They want God always to be answering their prayers, or they keep setting tests for God to demonstrate his concern for them, or they need regularly to be convinced that they are special to God. And the other sort of people are always doing their duty. They wouldn't dream of denting a commandment, far less breaking one, and they are ceaseless in the work they do for God. And when something unpleasant or painful happens, they ask: 'Why should this happen to me?', because all the time they have really been doing a deal with God, and God doesn't seem to have kept his side of the bargain. Which are you? Which am I?

The line between the prodigal son and his elder brother doesn't separate two different characters. It runs through each of us. Each of us wants the people we love to prove that they love us, and each of us wants God to do the same. We all try in our different ways to earn the love of someone else; and we all try to earn God's love too. Jesus was forever trying to get across to people: don't expect God to be proving all the time that he loves you. The birds of the air don't expect that, they just accept it. So why don't you? And Jesus was forever trying to show people that you can't buy God's love – which is why he said that those whom the conventionally respectable regarded as 'undesirable' would be first in the queue for the kingdom of heaven.

Paul once wrote: 'If God is for us, who is against us?' The strange thing is that it is those who had to struggle most to believe that God loves them, who find it most difficult to accept that they are accepted, who are most able to convince others that it is true. Like Paul. All his life, he wrestled with whether

God could really love so much that he loved him. All his life, he was trying to shake off his back the God who would only respond if Paul met his demands. Yet he summed it up in nine words in English – rather fewer in the Greek language in which he wrote to the church in Rome – 'If God is for us, who is against us?'

The journalist Alastair Moffat put the difference very clearly in a newspaper article about his mother and father: 'She loved us first and asked questions later. He asked questions, and if we supplied the right answers, then he might love us.' The God I believe in is the God without the 'if' clause.

Could Robert Burns have been thinking of the elder brother, so self-righteous, judgemental and critical, when he wrote 'An Epistle to the Unco Guid' (which just means the 'rigidly righteous')?

> Who made the heart, tis he alone
>     Decidedly can try us,
> He knows each chord its various tone,
>     Each spring its various bias;
> Then at the balance, let's be mute
>     We never can adjust it;
> What's done we partly may compute,
>     But know not what's resisted.

'I will get up and go to my father, and I will say to him: "Father, I have sinned against heaven and before you".'

In another poem which he wrote to a friend, Davie Sillar, Burns wrote:

> Nae treasures, nor pleasures
>     Could make us happy lang;

The heart ay's the part ay
    That makes us right or wrang.


'But while he was still far off, his father saw him, and his heart
went out to him.'

On holiday every year, in the East Neuk of Fife, we always
spend a very pleasant morning fruit-picking. If we start reasonably early in the morning before the sun really gets up, we can
in a couple of pleasant hours pick fruit to keep us (and a few of
our relatives) in jam through the rest of the year. Jesus once told
a story about men who were hired to go fruit-picking early in
the morning.

One morning on a visit to Israel, we left Jerusalem about
ten o'clock. The sun was already high and it was hot, not
oppressively hot but pleasant. In the big, air-conditioned car, we
chatted and joked and pointed out the sights we passed as we
drove not only northwards but downwards towards the Engedi
desert, and a long way below sea level, and then past Jericho
and along the Jordan valley to the Sea of Galilee. And when we
arrived at the hotel where we were staying, the car engine was
switched off, and with it the air-conditioning, and as soon as I
stepped out the oppressiveness of the heat was almost physical
in the way it hit me. It was only a few paces to the stairs leading
up to the hotel, but sweat was pouring from us all when we
reached the doors. And then inside, and the blessing once more
of air-conditioning. As we sat down, we reached an immediate
decision. We would work in the early morning, or the evening,
but not in the middle of the day.

Jesus once told a story about men who went fruit-picking
early in the morning, and had to work hard at it all day, right
through the oppressive heat of the noonday sun.

I am sometimes asked whether visits to the Holy Land make

any difference to my faith; and I usually say that if the question means do I have any sense, any experience of 'walking in the footsteps of the Master' (as the title of a famous book about the Holy Land puts it), then the answer is no. But I often see things or experience things which make parts of the Gospel come alive in a new way. And the sheer force of that heat hitting me made me understand the anger and the resentment of those in the story Jesus told about men who were hired to go fruit-picking early in the morning, and endured the heat and burden of the day, only to find that at the end of the day they were paid just the same as some others who had just done an hour's work in the cool of the evening.

That experience in the Holy Land helps me to understands the anger and resentment of the workers in the story. It makes the story come alive, if you like. But to understand the point of the story, we need to know something else. We need to know that there was a story very like the one Jesus told going the rounds of Palestine 2,000 years ago: about a king who hired a huge number of labourers. Two hours after work began, the king went to inspect their work, and he saw that one of them surpassed all the others in both skill and hard work. So he took him by the hand and walked up and down with him till the evening. When the labourers came to receive their wages, each of them received the same amount as all the others. And they complained to the king: 'We have worked the whole day, and this man only two hours, yet you have paid him the full day's wages'. The king replied: 'I have not wronged you; this labourer has done more in two hours than you have done during the whole day'.

It is almost exactly the story Jesus told, but with a very different punchline. 'This labourer has done more in two hours than you have done all day.' Payment by results. Cash on delivery. It is only natural justice. But in Jesus' story: 'I am not being unfair... You agreed on the usual wage... Surely I am free to do what I like with my own money'. It is nothing but divine generosity.

So many of the stories Jesus told are about a God who is nothing if not generous: the God who is like a king who does not just provide the bare necessities of life for his people, but lays on a banquet for them; the God who is like a father who does not just offer board and lodging to the son who returns home, but kills the fatted calf. The God who is like a travelling Samaritan, who does not just do the decent thing when he comes across a beaten-up man, stopping to make sure the man is all right, but takes him to the nearest inn and pays for his keep. The God who is like a merchant who collects fine pearls, and who does not just bargain and haggle over the price of the perfect one, but sells everything up and pays well over the odds because he wants it more than anything. The God who is like an employer who doesn't just measure out the wages in exact proportion to the work done, but who treats everyone equally. And the God who says, when we complain that it is not fair: 'Why be jealous because I am generous?' God's nature is always to be generous, and Jesus is his generosity for us.

Paul summed it up in a passage in the second letter he wrote to the Corinthians: 'You know the generosity of our Lord Jesus Christ; he was rich, yet for your sake he became poor, so that through his poverty we might become rich'. But there is something about generosity which makes us suspicious. Do we not sometimes talk about people being generous 'to a fault'? Is there not something about generous people which makes us wonder either if they might not be too good to be true, or else which makes us guilty when we are on the receiving end of their generosity?

When I was interviewing a television personality, in the

course of the conversation she told me how guilty she felt that she made so little effort to keep in touch with her friends, and yet whenever she met them again they never held it against her but simply welcomed her generously into their circle. And I said to her that maybe it was in the nature of generous friendship not to make demands, and maybe she should just accept what her friends offered without feeling guilt about it. And she said, a little testily: 'I know that's the theory, Johnston'.

When I was a very young assistant minister in St Giles' Cathedral, there was a very well-off old lady who took young assistants under her wing. She was extraordinarily generous to us, taking us to restaurants we would never dream of going to, buying us bottles of wine we could never afford on our tiny salaries, always on the look-out for ways to help. And whenever we protested at her kindness, she would say: 'Why do you find it so difficult to accept generosity?' If truth be told, it made us uncomfortable; and yet, why should it have?

Is there not something about God's generosity which we can't always accept without, perhaps, a lingering sense of doubt? There is something in us, something quite deep in all of us, I suspect, that finds it difficult to accept that God's acts of generosity don't have, hidden away somewhere, clauses in small print that mean we'll eventually have to pay for it.

Could it be because all of us, in our honest moments, know that it is very seldom that we are genuinely generous, honestly open-handed, capable of giving without counting the cost or working for others without seeking any reward (as Ignatius Loyola's famous 'Prayer for Generosity' puts it)? And so we find it difficult to imagine even Almighty God behaving so differently from us. And yet, do we not believe that we have been made in God's image, made to be generous in the image of a generous God?

In Luke's Gospel, Jesus says: 'Be compassionate, be generous, just as your Father is compassionate and generous'. So, Jesus says, do not judge; do not condemn; be forgiving, and again, he says, be generous. And then Jesus says that strange thing about taking the plank out of your own eye before you try to take the speck out of someone else's eye. The Jewish people of Jesus' day had a phrase they used about a good eye and a bad eye, and they did not just mean an eye that sees well and an eye that is out of focus. They had noticed, these people of Jesus' day, that mean people screwed up their eyes when they were going to refuse to do you a favour, and a generous person was wide-eyed when granting a request. In fact, they used the phrase 'a good eye' when we would say 'an open hand'. Jesus has been speaking about generosity – the generosity which is what marks us out as made in the image of God. And, he says, don't judge; especially, don't judge someone else's generosity. For how can you see the fault in their eye, their lack of generosity, unless your own eye is clear, unless you yourself are generous?

So, very early on the morning after we arrived in scorching Galilee, we made our way to a beautiful church by the shores of the Sea of Galilee. It's called 'The Church of the Multiplication' because it is built on what is traditionally thought to be the place where Jesus fed the 5,000 – the multiplication of the loaves and fishes. God's generosity in action. Inside the church, there are ancient medieval mosaics, representing Christian symbols: loaves and fishes, and on one side of the altar a pelican. Why a pelican? Well, certainly not because of the modern lines that

A magnificent bird is the pelican
Its beak can hold more than its belly can

– but rather because of the ancient belief that the mother pelican pecked her breast with her beak in order to feed her young with her own blood. It's not actually biologically accurate. But, as a symbol of the sacrificial generosity of God, it's as powerful as it is true.

When religious broadcasting began, the Bible was never used in broadcasts because the General Post Office, which was responsible for transmitting the broadcast signals, had insisted that matters of controversy should not be broadcast! Nowadays, when people in broadcasts say things which are controversial, on the basis of what they have read in the Bible, I am likely to receive letters asking whether I do not remember that Jesus said: 'Render to Caesar what is Caesar's, and to God what is God's'. In other words, religious broadcasters should stick to talking about spiritual matters. But the trouble with something as general as rendering to Caesar what is Caesar's and to God what is God's is that we are left to choose for ourselves what is Caesar's and what is God's. And where I draw the line will be different from where you draw the line. So, to say to people that they should give Caesar what is Caesar's and God what is God's is not really a very helpful piece of advice.

But I do not think Jesus was in the business of handing down pieces of advice. He did not deal in generalities or abstract principles. When he was asked by a smart young lawyer who his neighbour was, Jesus did not just say something about the duty each of us owes to each other; he told a very specific story about a dangerous road, a traveller and a Samaritan. When someone wanted him to intervene in a dispute between two brothers about property, he did not just warn one of the brothers about greed; he told a very specific story about a man building bigger and bigger barns. When some people criticised him for the company he kept, he did not just make a state-ment about everyone being equal in the sight of God; he told a very specific story about a shepherd going searching for a lost sheep.

So, when he said: 'Render to Caesar the things that are Caesar's and to God the things that are God's', what specifically could Jesus have had in mind? As far as I can tell, there is only one occasion in the Gospels when Jesus actually talks very specifically about a duty which people owed to Caesar, to the Roman army of occupation, where Jesus says: 'If someone in authority presses you into service for one mile, go with him two'. A Roman soldier, in the name of the Emperor, was entitled to force anyone to carry his pack for a mile. A Roman official, in the name of the Emperor, was entitled to requisition someone's transport for a mile. And Jesus says that, if that happens, do not just go the first mile, which is what you owe to Caesar. Go the extra mile. That is what you owe to God. The first mile renders to Caesar what is Caesar's; the extra mile, because it meets oppression with kindness, and legal demand with abundant generosity, and judicial sanctions with prodigal compassion, renders to God what is God's.

A few years ago, I spent a week in Bosnia with a Territorial Army chaplain, Jim Gibson, and the soldiers to whom he ministered at a place called Sipovo high in the hills. One day, the Croats had come over the hill and told the 10,000 or so inhabitants they had thirty minutes to leave the village or they would be shot. So they became refugees. Then the Serbs came, and the Croats had to leave; but, before they did so, they destroyed many of the houses. The people of Sipovo came back to shells of their former homes. And many of them were still living in the shells. The winter was getting close. The snow would come and stay, and the conditions in which the soldiers were living were far from comfortable. But that is their job, and they are paid for it and they did not complain.

Where they go the second mile and a good deal more is when some of them encounter a family with little or no food and they dig into their own pockets to provide it. A budget of £300 a month from the reconstruction fund does not go far. So, soldiers are supplementing it out of their own pockets. Where they go the second mile is when a couple of young privates, one from Galashiels and the other from Gourock, start writing letters to firms asking for donations of toys or chocolates so that the children of Sipovo can have the Christmas they would not have without help. There's 80 per cent unemployment and no unemployment benefit. I doubt if any of these soldiers would use religious language; indeed, the language a lot of them use is far from religious. But it is going the second mile, far beyond the call of duty you might say – going the extra mile.

It is what is extra that is God's due. What is extra. But that is just another generalisation, another principle to be put into effect. So, can we be more specific than that? Going the extra mile when nobody can actually force you to do so is an extravagant gesture. So, maybe what we're expected to render to God is extravagance; and, if we turn to the Gospels, there are two passages which spell out what extravagance in the cause of the Gospel is all about.

Jesus is in the house of Simon the leper. As he reclines at table, a woman comes in carrying a bottle of very costly perfume, and she breaks the top of the bottle off, and pours all the contents over Jesus' head. Some of those present say indignantly: 'What a waste. The perfume could have been sold for the equivalent of a year's pay, and the money given to the poor.' Why the waste? Why the extravagance? The American poet Robinson Jeffers writes:

Is it not by his high superfluousness we know
our God? For to *equal* a need

is natural, animal, mineral: but to fling
rainbows over the rain,
and beauty above the moon, and secret rainbows
on the domes of deep sea shells,
and make the necessary embrace of breeding
beautiful also as fire,
nor even the weeds to multiply without blossom,
nor the birds without music . . .
the extravagant kindness of God.

In the other passage which for me spells out the sort of extravagance which responds to an extravagant God, Jesus is walking by the sea of Galilee when he comes across some fishermen in their boat by the shore. They tell him they've been fishing all night without success. They are frustrated and disappointed, as well as probably cold and wet. 'Put out into deep water, and let down your nets for a catch', Jesus tells them. 'Launch out into the deep.'

They had to push the boat out, which is what we say when someone is indulging in an extravagant gesture. 'Let's push the boat out tonight' – and splash out on a celebration, or a party or a special occasion. 'Let's push the boat out.' So these fishermen pushed the boat out into deep water, and they found, in the company of that stranger, that all their ideas about themselves and the world and their place in it, all their notions about God and their people and God's plans for them . . . all were ground down, confused and mixed up, and remade and reformed in the company of this stranger. T. S. Eliot says:

Let me tell you that to approach the stranger
Is to invite the unexpected, release a new force,
Or let the genie out of the bottle.

It is to start a train of events
Beyond your control.

It is about taking an extravagant risk, faith. For you have no idea what cherished notions you may have to throw overboard because they just do not seem to hold water any more, out there, in the deep. And hope is about taking an extravagant risk too. For there are none of the familiar landmarks that you were able to steer by when you hugged the shore and stayed in the shallows. Maybe there is just one guiding star and you have to hope it's the right one. And love is about taking an extravagant risk too. For love very quickly gets out of its depth, if it's truly love at all, and it takes the incredible risk that it can endure everything and not be quenched even by many waters.

Thomas Carlyle once said that when a ship returns to port, 'granted the ship comes into harbour with shrouds and tackle damaged; the pilot is blameworthy; he has not been all-wise and all-powerful; but to know *how* blameworthy, tell us first whether his voyage has been round the Globe, or only to Ramsgate and the Isle of Dogs'! To take the risk of faith is to render to God what belongs to God who took the extravagant risk of believing in us, becoming one with us, being dependent on us. Render to Caesar the things that are Caesar's, and to God the things that are God's. Most of us are decent, upright citizens, rendering to Caesar precisely what is Caesar's. But Jesus said once: what is there *extraordinary* about that?

# 11

# Travelling Hopefully

NOWADAYS there are sophisticated, well-organised, carefully thought-out selection procedures designed to decide who will and who will not make good ministers of the Church; but, in the days when I decided I would like to be a minister, it was all very different. You filled in a form, had a chat with a couple of local ministers, and, if they agreed, then your name was put before a committee in Edinburgh which decided whether you could be an approved student for the ministry.

Just before my application was due to be considered by the Edinburgh committee, I came home from a day at university to find my father in his study chatting with another minister, who happened to be one of the Edinburgh committee. 'What are you going to do when you graduate?', this other minister asked me. I muttered something about becoming a minister, and waited for the usual speech about 'following in father's footsteps' and then for my father's usual speech about 'never being half the man his father is'. I had been through it all many times before. But this time it was different. My father said: 'He's a fool. He should learn from his father's mistakes. He could make much more money doing all sorts of other things, and I've told him as much. But he's a fool, and he won't listen to advice.' I should add that my father had a perverse sense of humour which a lot of people, including the other minister, did not appreciate. So my father's visitor told me that he could not think of anything better than becoming a minister, and he would be delighted to speak up for me at the Edinburgh committee. Only long after-wards did I discover that, when my name came up at the com-mittee, this minister said that I should be given all the support possible because I was wanting to go into the ministry in spite of enormous parental opposition! So I got through because my father said I was a fool.

More than once, Paul described himself as a fool; and it's even less complimentary in the original Greek, because the word Paul wrote for 'fool' was the Greek word *moron*. In one sense, however, Paul was nobody's fool. He was not above parading his academic credentials in his letters: how he had studied under the great Gamaliel, and had forgotten more of his legal training than his critics had ever learned. But, in his first letter to the church at Corinth, he calls himself 'a fool for Christ's sake'. He was being sarcastic, of course, speaking in jest; but there is many a true word spoken in jest.

Kings and queens used to keep jesters, or fools. Mary Queen of Scots kept one; and, while most of the men in her life came to a sad end, as she did – one husband, Lord Darnley, and her alleged lover David Rizzio were both murdered, while another husband, the Earl of Bothwell, died in a Danish prison – one powerful influence in her life survived: her fool, Jamie Geddes. Kings and queens did not keep jesters because they wanted to be amused. Fools were not comedians. They belonged to the court, but they were not part of the court. Fools were not part of the scheming and the plotting, the manoeuvring and the manipulation, the jockeying for position and the struggle for power. And so fools saw things which other people did not see, and they said things which other people could not say. They got away with speaking the truth. Indeed, fools were the only people the king or queen could trust to speak the truth, because everyone knew that the fool was not out for his own gain. After all, he was just a fool. Fools for Christ's sake? In that sense, Paul's sarcasm was to contain an insight he did not intend.

That great religious journalist Gerald Priestland once asked the question: who needs the Church? And he answered: 'The man in the street needs the Church. The greatest single reason why the man in the street needs the Church is that he needs an alternative source of criticism and comment on the way the world works.' The world needs Christians, not to be committed to the world's ways, but to say the foolish things, the true things, which perhaps only Christians will say because they are not, or they should not be, part of the way the world works. That is a very difficult balance for Christians to strike. It is possible to become so involved with the world which God loves that we become immersed in it and indistinguishable from it; and that's the temptation to be absorbed. However, sometimes in avoiding that temptation, Christians become what someone has called 'unconvincing salesmen for the world to come', and that is the temptation to be irrelevant. The way of the fool is to take the way the world works seriously enough to see through it, but not so seriously that we get caught up in its futile obsessions with status and power and success.

Fools for Christ's sake? The modern counterpart of the fool is, I suppose, the clown. Colin Morris, who reached positions of great distinction both in the Methodist Church and in the BBC, asks in one of his books:

Why do clowns make us laugh? Because they are foolish enough to refuse to conform to the limits of the possible. The clown insists on riding a bicycle whose wheels are out of kilter. The clown tries to walk along a slack tightrope. It can't be done but the clown is always absurdly attempting the impossible. Dozens of times, in film after film, Charlie

Chaplin would go up to the bully with a smile on his face and his hand outstretched, only to be punched on the nose for his trouble. But he just dusts himself down, like the clown who falls off the ridiculous bicycle, and starts all over again, finding endless excuses for those who cause him pain.[21]

Fools for Christ's sake? Jesus of Nazareth refused to allow people to conform to the limits of the possible. 'Stretch out your hand', he says to a man who has never had the use of his arm. It is impossible. 'Get up and walk', he says to a man who has never taken a step in his life. It is impossible. 'Join me in Galilee', he says to men and women who are paralysed with fear. It is impossible. A miracle happens not when the impossible becomes possible. A miracle happens when the impossible remains impossible and yet happens. So, Christians are committed to a vision of the impossible, which will only be realised by people who are foolish enough to believe that it can happen. Like the clown, Christians are meant to live out their dreams.

Fools for Christ's sake? What else should we be if we are to follow someone who talked about and practised absurdities like loving your enemies, who cherished the unlovable and the unlovely, and who claimed that forgiving and being forgiven is what makes us really human? I do not know how many speeches I have heard in the nearly forty years that I have attended the annual meeting of the Church of Scotland General Assembly; but the one I remember best was by the great churchman Archie Craig. He got to his feet after a typical speech by George MacLeod, Lord MacLeod of Fuinary. 'What I have just heard', Archie Craig said, 'is intemperate, impractical and irrational, and for these reasons I want to support it. Because in these characteristics I recognise the authentic voice of Jesus of Nazareth.'

A couple of years ago, I was interviewing a church leader about how the Gospel might change the world through the foolishness of God which is wiser than men, and he said to me: 'But there's a real world out there'. Well, in that real world, only a fool would say that ultimately it is the poor in spirit who matter. Only a fool would say that gentleness is what will inherit the earth. Only a fool would say that you find happiness through forgiving. Only a fool would say that making peace and suffering persecution are so inextricably linked that they will both be rewarded equally. If being a fool means turning the world's idea of truth on its head and offering it the absurdity which makes sense, and if being a fool means refusing to accept the conventional limits of what is possible, then Jesus of Nazareth was a fool. And maybe it was a fool's paradise that he promised to those who followed him. But rather fools in that paradise with him, than wise in the world that works so badly.

One of my sons was born when I was a parish minister in Glasgow. When he was taken out in his pram, more than one member of my congregation said to me: 'Well, you can't deny that one'. Apart from the implication that I was regularly in the position of having to deny paternity, I think what people meant was that Robert is very like me. And so he is. But what does it mean to say that you and I and all of us are made 'in the likeness of God'? Clearly, it does not mean that, physically, we are made in the likeness of God, as if to say that God has eyes and ears and hands and feet, although I am perfectly happy to talk about 'God's eyes' and 'God's ears' and 'God's hands' – because what language do we have other than human language to use of God?

When the great nineteenth-century theologian John MacLeod Campbell was tried for heresy by the Church of Scotland and found guilty, all because he taught that 'God loved everyone with a love the measure of which was the death of his own son' – these are John MacLeod Campbell's own words, and they had him deposed from the ministry of the Church of Scotland – at his trial, his father, by then aged over 80, spoke in his defence, and his last words were: 'Though his brethren cast him out, his Master whom he serves will not forsake him; and while I live I will never be ashamed to be the father of so blameless a son'. One of the reasons John MacLeod Campbell was so convinced that God could not behave in the way the orthodox of his day believed:

Sending ane to heaven and ten tae hell
A' for thy glory

was that he could not imagine God behaving in a less loving and compassionate way than his own father, with whom he had such a close relationship. He was someone who allowed the best in our human relationships to illustrate what was natural in our relationship with God; and, in describing God, we have only human experiences, human language, which may be inadequate – of course it is – but it is the only language we've got. So, even though we know God has no eyes, it is still helpful to talk about what God sees. Even though we know God has no ears, it still make sense to talk about God hearing. Even though we know God does not have hands, it still communicates to say that we are all of us in them.

But, if we do not share physical features with God, what does it mean to say that we are made 'in his likeness'? I think it's possible to identify at least three ways that we are made in the likeness of God.

First of all, God is the creator; and we are creative too. When we think of God's creativity, we get far too hung up, I think, on how everything began. It is all the fault of the Creed, I suppose. The first thing the Creed says about God is: 'maker of heaven and earth', and somehow that gets it into our head that that is what God's creativity is all about. In one of his sermons, Andrew McLellan says this: 'Creating is what God is always doing, making things new, making things lovely . . . Rebuilding lives after disaster. Picking up the pieces after disappointment. Opening doors after failure. These are some of the ways God's creative face is shown to us.' They are, and they are at least as much creative moments as that moment which the Book of Genesis begins to describe 'in the beginning'. I would go so far as to say these moments are more typical of God's creativity because they involve working with and through and in people.

The former Archbishop of York, John Habgood, makes the point in one of his books. He quotes the elder brother of Michael Ramsey, the former Archbishop of Canterbury. Frank Ramsey was a healthy-minded unbeliever who once wrote: 'I don't feel in the least humble before the vastness of the heavens. The stars may be large, but they cannot think or love; and these are qualities which impress me far more than size does. I take no credit for weighing more than seventeen stones.' To be constantly making all things new, creating and recreating loving relationships, and hopeful encounters and faithful consciences, is much more characteristic of God's creativity than the sun and the moon and the stars!

To explore a second way in which we are made in the likeness of God, I want to use another translation of 'made in the likeness of God', namely 'made in the image of God'. Because we are made in the image of God, we have imaginations. Because God is imaginative. The Scottish theologian John McIntyre has written a book about faith and imagination, and I want to share three ideas from that book. First of all, he

says, we should be concerned for the world around us, for con-
servation, for ecology, not just because the world's resources
need to be conserved but because *the beauty of the earth* has
been imaginatively and profusely loaded with such splendour
by God. Second, the imaginative creativity which God showed
in forming the world about us, he demonstrated again in the
coming of Jesus, an event so unexpected, so unpredictable and
so imaginative that those around Jesus failed to recognise what
was happening because it was too imaginative. The seventeenth-
century French theologian Pascal once asked the question:
'Must Christ die in every generation to save those who have no
imagination?' So, made in the image of God, we share in God's
creativity when we use our imaginations.

But it is the third thing which John McIntyre says that really
made me sit up and take notice. He says that imagination is an
essential part of love. God so loved the world. It takes divine
imagination to see the world as lovable, to see sinners as
redeemable, to see humanity as renewable. When the divine
imagination took human flesh, Jesus, God's imagination at
work saw potential where everyone else saw only failure. That
is the story of his dealings with people from Zacchaeus to Peter
by way of Mary Magdalene. God's imagination saw beyond
what everyone else was content to accept, to what with him
could be achieved. That too is the story of his dealings with
people from Lazarus to Jairus' daughter by way of Peter's wife's
mother. God's imagination saw behind surface and sometimes
flattering responses to the reality of people's commitment. That
was true from the day when Jesus fed the 5,000 and they wanted
to make him king and he escaped in a boat to the procession
through the streets of Jerusalem on Palm Sunday when they
shouted hosanna and he wept over the city.

All of that required divine imagination: to see through and

beyond and behind the appearance of very unpromising people and situations to what could be promises fulfilled and situations transformed. So, you and I, who are called to love the world, our neighbour as ourselves, can only do that if we have the imagination to see in people what the casual observer will not notice and the self-centred individual will ignore, and what hidebound systems and policies and strategies and organisations cannot cope with – hidden loveliness and unrecognisable talent and overgrown freshness and beauty that's more than skin deep. We show that we are made in God's image when we share God's imaginative love. And we show that we are made in God's image when we share God's extravagant generosity. 'Be generous, as your father in heaven is generous.'

Some time ago, my wife and daughter and I went to Sung Eucharist in King's College Chapel in Cambridge. And as we sat waiting for the service to begin, and I looked again round that extravagantly beautiful building, I remembered being told that it was built when King's College had only seventy students. But it was built not to house seventy students but to the glory of God, reckless in extravagant beauty and poured out in uncalculated love to God. When the poet William Wordsworth visited King's College in Cambridge, that's what caught his imagination too.

Give all thou canst; high Heaven rejects the lore
Of nicely calculated less or more.
So deemed the man who fashioned for the sense
These lofty pillars, spread that branching roof
Self-poised, and scooped into ten thousand cells
Where light and shade repose, where music dwells.

Ignatius Loyola called his prayer – about giving and not counting the cost, and toiling and not seeking for rest, and labouring and not asking for any reward – 'A Prayer for Generosity'. I quoted it on an occasion when I had to preach at a service for the induction of a new minister in Glasgow, and a very distinguished minister told me afterwards that he had always thought giving and not counting the cost was a recipe for bankruptcy, and toiling and not seeking for rest just led to a nervous breakdown, and labouring without asking for any reward was economic madness – and of course all of that's right, which is why lawyers will always make much more successful churchmen than poets!

Richard Holloway says that what never fails to move him to tears are when he experiences acts of unmerited generosity. And one of the stories that people have told, about what was happening when Jesus died on the cross, is that it was an act of generosity, of boundless generosity on the part of God – God so loved the world that he gave his only son – that when we realised just how unmerited it was, we would be moved. Love so amazing so divine, demands my soul, my life, my all. When Isaac Watts wrote that, he didn't mean that love actively demanded anything, but that the demand was felt in us that nothing was too good or too precious to withhold.

John Bunyan wrote:

A man there was, though some did count him mad,
The more he cast away, the more he had.

We are made in the image of God, in the likeness of the one whom Paul described also as 'the image of God'.

# Notes

1. Robert Davidson, *The Courage to Doubt* (SCM, 1983).
2. Rosalind Galt, 'Letter from New York', *The Scottish Review* (Winter 2001–2).
3. Rowan Williams, *Writing in the Dust* (Hodder & Stoughton, 2002).
4. Brendan Kennelly, *The Book of Judas* (Bloodaxe, 1991), p. 268.
5. William Klassen, *Judas: Betrayer or Friend of Jesus?* (SCM, 1996).
6. James A. Whyte, *Laughter and Tears* (Saint Andrew Press, 1993), p. 94.
7. J. Leslie Houlden, *Backward into Light* (SCM, 1987).
8. Professor John O'Neill first pointed this out to me as a student of his in the 1960s.
9. Lord Hailsham, *A Sparrow's Flight* (HarperCollins/Fontana, 1990), p. 403.
10. Richard Holloway, *Let God Arise* (Mowbray, 1972), p. 70.
11. Andrew Barr, 'Mission Impossible? Televising Worship', a paper written for the General Synod of the Church of England, February 2002.
12. Alistair Kee, *From Bad Faith to Good News* (SCM, 1991), pp. 44–5.
13. I owe this reference to my friend Rev. Bob Brown, who used it in a radio broadcast.
14. I owe this story to Rev. Dr John Munro, who told it on a *Thought for the Day* on BBC Radio Scotland.
15. Taken from *The Story of the Atonement* by Stephen Sykes, published and copyright © 1997 by Darton, Longman & Todd Ltd, and used by permission of the publishers.
16. George MacLeod, quoted in Kathy Galloway, *Love Burning Deep* (SPCK, 1993).
17. G. A. Studdert Kennedy, 'He Was a Gambler Too', *The Unutterable Beauty* (Hodder & Stoughton, 1968 edn, first published 1927).
18. Taken from *Resurrection* by Rowan Williams, published and copyright © 1982 by Darton, Longman & Todd Ltd, and used by permission of the publishers.

19. Edward Shillito, 'Jesus of the Scars'.
20. 'Sheaves', *Its Colours They Are Fine* (© 1999 Alan Spence, reproduced by
    kind permission of HarperCollins Publishers Ltd).
21. Colin Morris, *The Hammer of the Lord* (Epworth, 1973), p. 91.

# Acknowledgements

pp. xii–xiii 'A Good Man in Hell' by Edwin Muir, published by Faber & Faber Ltd, reproduced by kind permission of the publisher.

p. 33 'The Killing' by Edwin Muir, published by Faber & Faber Ltd, reproduced by kind permission of the publisher.

p. 55 Taken from *Murder in the Cathedral* by T. S. Eliot, published by Faber & Faber Ltd, reproduced by kind permission of the publisher.

pp. 77–8 'Lord of all hopefulness'. Words by Jan Struther (1901–53) from 'Enlarged Songs of Praise 1931' by permission of Oxford University Press.

pp. 103–4 Sydney Carter 'The Present Tense', copyright © Stainer & Bell Ltd, London, England. Reproduced from 'The two-way clock'.

p. 115 Taken from 'Choruses from The Rock' from *Collected Poems 1909–1962* by T. S. Eliot, published by Faber & Faber Ltd, reproduced by kind permission of the publisher.

p. 142 'Walking Away' by C. Day Lewis: *The Complete Poems* by C. Day Lewis, published by Sinclair-Stevenson (1992), copyright © 1992 in this edition, and the Estate of C. Day Lewis.

pp. 159–60 Taken from 'The Cocktail Party' by T. S. Eliot, published by Faber & Faber Ltd, reproduced by kind permission of the publisher.

173